Richard Warner

The History of the Isle of Wight

Military, Ecclesiastical, Civil, & Natural

Richard Warner

The History of the Isle of Wight
Military, Ecclesiastical, Civil, & Natural

ISBN/EAN: 9783744724562

Printed in Europe, USA, Canada, Australia, Japan

Cover: Foto ©ninafisch / pixelio.de

More available books at **www.hansebooks.com**

THE

HISTORY

OF THE

ISLE OF WIGHT;

MILITARY,

ECCLESIASTICAL, CIVIL, & NATURAL:

TO WHICH IS ADDED

A VIEW OF ITS AGRICULTURE.

By the Rev. RICHARD WARNER;

EDITOR OF
"HAMPSHIRE EXTRACTED FROM DOMESDAY BOOK," AND OF
THE "ANTIQUITATES CULINARIÆ;"
AND AUTHOR OF
"TOPOGRAPHICAL REMARKS RELATING TO HAMPSHIRE," AND
"AN ATTEMPT TO ASCERTAIN THE SITUATION OF
THE ANCIENT CLAUSENTUM."

" Tu nimio nec stricta gelu, nec sidere fervens,
Clementi cœlo, temperieque places.
Cum pareret Natura parens varioque favore
Divideret dotes omnibus una locis,
Seposuit potiora tibi, macremque professa,
' Insula sis felix, plenaque pacis' ait.
' Quicquid amat luxus, quicquid desiderat usus,
Ex te provenier, vel aliundè tibi.' "

SOUTHAMPTON,
PRINTED FOR T. CADELL, JUN. AND W. DAVIES, (SUCCESSORS
TO MR. CADELL) IN THE STRAND, LONDON;
AND T. BAKER, SOUTHAMPTON.

MDCCXCV.

TO

SIR WILLIAM HEATHCOTE, BART.

AND

WILLIAM CHUTE, ESQ.

MEMBERS FOR THE COUNTY OF HANTS,

SIR HARRY BURRARD, BART.

GEORGE ROSE, ESQ.

JAMES MOWBRAY, ESQ.

AND

THE REV. WILLIAM GILPIN,

THE FOLLOWING EPITOMIZED

HISTORY OF THE ISLE OF WIGHT,

IS GRATEFULLY INSCRIBED,

BY THEIR OBEDIENT

AND OBLIGED

HUMBLE SERVANT,

R. WARNER, JUN.

ADVERTISEMENT.

SEVERAL publications have already appeared relative to the Iſle of Wight. It will therefore be naturally expected, that the author of the preſent one either produce ſomething *new* on the ſubject, or preſent the materials before offered to the public, in a different and improved form.

Both theſe objects it has been his endeavour to attain; with what ſucceſs the reader will beſt pronounce.

Frequent

Frequent visits to the island, and habitual propensities,* allowed him opportunity and inclination to make some collections relative to its natural history; and a conviction that very little information of this kind had hitherto been given to the world, inspired the hope of his collections carrying at least the recommendation of *novelty* with them, should he methodize and publish them. This he at length determined to do; adding, at the same time, to his plan, a luminous and methodical, but concise detail, of the principal circumstances in

* " ητι εγωγε
Ης γαιης δυναμαι γλυκερωτερον αλλο ιδεσθαι."—Hom. Odyss.

To me no fond pursuits such pleasures yield,
As the gay scenes of *Nature's* varied field.

the

the military, ecclefiaftical, and civil hiftory of the ifland.

He would not, however, be underſtood to have attempted a *complete natural hiſtory* of the Iſle of Wight, in the following pages. He wiſhes them to be confidered rather as an *index*, which fome future *fauniſt* may improve and amplify. An *accurate* natural hiſtory of this varied and extenſive diſtrict, would, of itſelf, form a very bulky volume; fo large an one, as perhaps the abilities and leiſure of no ſingle individual would allow him to complete. The ſubject is fo unbounded, and Nature fo inexhauſtible, that, even after all his labors, he muſt find much remained undone; and be content at laſt to allow the truth of the Philo-

fopher's

sopher's" observation : " *Multum adhuc restat operis, multumque restabit; nec ulli nato post mille secula præcludetur occasio aliquid adhuc adjiciendi.*"*

* L. A. Seneca, Epist. lxiv.

CONTENTS.

The Military History of the Isle of Wight.

CHAP. I.

Of the original inhabitants of the Isle of Wight   PAGE 1

CHAP. II.

Of the Romans, in the Isle of Wight - - 8

CHAP. III.

Of the Saxons, in the Isle of Wight - - 16

CHAP. IV.

Of the Danes and Normans, in the Isle of Wight - - - - - - - 24

CHAP. V.

Military history of the island, from Edward I. to the present time - - - - - 36

CHAP. VI.

The ancient and present defence of the Isle of Wight - - - - - - - 54

The Ecclesiastical History of the Isle of Wight.

CHAP. I.

Of the ancient religion of the Isle of Wight, and the introduction of Christianity there - 87

CHAP. II.

Of the religious foundations in the Isle of Wight 98

The Civil History of the Isle of Wight.

CHAP. I.

Of the boroughs of Newport, Newtown, and Yarmouth - - - - - - 129

CHAP. II.

Of the lords of the island; their power, rights, and franchises; and of the Knighton Court 147

CHAP. III.

Of the wardens, captains, and governors of the island - - - - - - 154

The Natural History of the Isle of Wight.

CHAP. I.

General description of the island; climate; soil; timber; rivers; springs; inhabitants; downs; and curious particulars relating to them - - - - - - - 167

CHAP. II.

Of the ancient connection of the Isle of Wight with the main land; its coast; rocks; caverns; chines, &c. - - - - - - 186

CHAP. III.

The zoology of the Isle of Wight; its animals, reptiles, and fish - - - - - 203

CHAP. IV.

The ornithology of the island - - - - 225

CHAP. V.

Of the botany of the island - - - - 247

CHAP. VI.

Of the fossilogy of the island - - - - 256

A General

A General View of the Agriculture of the Isle of Wight.

CHAP. I.
A sketch of the progress of agriculture in Britain, from the earliest to the present times. 265

CHAP. II.
Of the different grains sown; usual course of crops; various manures, &c. - - - 273

CHAP. III.
Turnips; grasses; pasture; draining; and roads 285

CHAP. IV.
Sheep, horses, cows, and swine - - - 288

CHAP. V.
Waste-land; forests; and sea-mud - - 293

CHAP. VI.
Improvements and experiments - - - 300

CHAP. VII.
The poor; laborers; and rates of wages - 305

APPENDIX.

APPENDIX.

A Differtation on Six Roman Coins - - 1

A copy of the Rate made for the Maintenance
of the Minifter of Newport - - - 13

PLATES.

Map - - - - - to face title-page
Needle Rocks - - - - - 200
Coins - - - - (appendix) 1

THE

MILITARY HISTORY

OF THE

ISLE OF WIGHT.

CHAP. I.

OF THE ORIGINAL INHABITANTS OF THE
ISLE OF WIGHT.

THE imperfect light which glimmers on the early antiquities of Britain, is chiefly imparted by the writings of the Greeks and Romans.

From these sources of intelligence we collect, that the Aboriginal inhabitants of this kingdom were a tribe of the Celtæ, Galatæ, or Gauls,

(descendants

(defcendants of the Gomerians, or Phrygians) who migrated hither from the coaft of Gaul.*

At what period they performed this migration, cannot, perhaps, be *exactly* afcertained; though it feems likely to have happened about one thoufand years before the Chriftian Æra.†

The Kentifh fhore would probably be the fpot which firft received thefe wanderers, on account of its vicinity to the regions from whence they came. They would not, however, long confine themfelves to this corner of the kingdom; the preffure of additional emigrants would oblige them to feek more diftant habitations, and they would foon extend themfelves along the Southern and Eaftern coafts of the country. This would probably happen about a century after the arrival of the original tribe; at which period we may fuppofe the Ifle of Wight received its firft inhabitants.

* Tacitus, de Vit. Agric. c. xi. Strabo, lib. II. et Cæfar, lib. V.

† Whitaker's Hift. Manchefter, b. I. c. i. p. 7.

Thefe

These *Aborigines* do not seem to have been far removed from the rudest state of savage life; they were barbarous and unenlightened; having no fixed habitations; wandering from place to place; and subsisting chiefly by the labours of the chace.*

After these wild tribes had continued about five centuries in their acquisitions, another host of wanderers, to whom historians give the appellation of Belgæ, deserted their own country, *Gallia Belgica*, crossed the strait that separated them from Britain, and began to disperse themselves through the Southern shores of the kingdom. A people, who, though originally a *Celtic* tribe, were not marked by the same ferocious characteristics with their ancestors, but were more cultivated and refined; more civilized in their manners, and comfortable in their modes of life.

It is not to be supposed, however, that these new visitors would gain an immediate, or a peaceable possession of the district, to which

* Cæsar, lib. V.

accident, curiosity, or distress, had led them. Every inch of territory was obstinately disputed, and many a bloody battle fought, ere the surly Britons were driven by their successful invaders into the interior, and more retired parts of the country. At length the Belgæ succeeded, and before the period of Cæsar's arrival in Britain, the whole Southern coast was in the possession of this warlike tribe.

The Isle of Wight had, doubtless, been deeply affected by this great and general revolution; and, at least a century before the Christian Æra, had received, in the room of its sordid and barbarous inhabitants, a race of people who already understood and practised the arts of husbandry and commerce.*

In their possession, it soon began to assume a more comfortable appearance than it had hitherto exhibited; villages and towns† were built, and its ports visited by foreign traders.

* Cæsar, ut supra.
† It seems likely that a British town, or city, stood on, or near the spot of the present Carisbrook; for *Caer broc* (the probable *original* name) is a Celtic compound, signifying the city or town of yew trees.

The

The daring spirit of the Phœnician navigators, had led them to the South-Weſtern promontories of Britain, about four centuries before the birth of our Saviour.* Here they found an article of traffic, rare and uſeful; and immediately entered into a commercial correſpondence with the Belerian Britons, for the purchaſe of the *tin*, which was produced in large quantities in the iſlands of Cornwall. †

For upwards of two hundred years did the merchants of Tyre and Carthage preſerve the monopoly of this lucrative trade, notwithſtanding the conſtant endeavours of all the other Mediterranean powers to diſcover and participate it.‡ The Greeks of Marſeilles, however, at

* Herodotus, Weſſelingii, p. 254.

† Pliny, lib. VII. c. lvi. The Scilly Iſlands received their ancient appellation of *Caſſiterides*, from the circumſtance of their yielding this valuable metal; from the Greek, Κασσιτερος, *tin*.

‡ So careful were the Phœnicians in concealing the courſe of the veſſels employed in this trade, that the captain of one of them, perceiving he was purſued by a Roman galley, in order to find out to what part he was bound, immediately *ſunk his bark*, to prevent the diſcovery. Strabo, p. 265.

length

length traced out the secret, and about two centuries prior to the Christian Æra, began to avail themselves of it. From this period the Carthaginian commerce dwindled away, and the Massylian daily extended itself; but as the latter people were by no means such experienced seamen as the mariners of Phœnicia, and consequently less able to encounter the stormy seas of the Belerian coast, the mode of traffic was (probably at the solicitation of the Greeks, and by the consent of the Britons) somewhat changed; and the staple of tin removed from the Western extremity of the kingdom, to the Southern shore; and fixed in the Isle of Wight, or, (according to the name by which it was known to the Marseillese) in the Island Ictis.*

The foreign traders were now no longer at the trouble of performing a tedious and dangerous voyage; but employing the *Veneti* of Gaul to transport the commodity from the new emporium to the opposite shore, they there received it, and sent it over land to Narbonne and Marseilles.†

* Diodorus Siculus, p. 347. † Strabo, 297.

We may fairly suppose that the Isle of Wight now began to rise into consideration.—The resort of foreign merchants to its ports, would introduce a degree of civilization among its inhabitants, hitherto unknown on the Southern shores of Britain. A rapid progress would be made in all the necessary arts of life. Improvements would be adopted in the civil polity of the people; and the whole district would soon smile with wealth, comfort, and prosperity.

CHAP.

CHAP. II.

OF THE ROMANS, IN THE ISLE OF WIGHT.

THE expeditions of Cæsar into Britain cannot be confidered as amounting to a conqueft of the country. His firft defcent was little more than a difcovery of it.* The fucceffes alfo which attended his fecond, were confined only to the South-Eaftern corner of the ifland, and gave to the Romans neither a firm footing, nor durable authority in it. To complete the reduction of our anceftors, and bring them under the Roman yoke, was a tafk left for Claudius to perform; which, by himfelf and his lieutenants,

* "Igitur primus omnium Romanorum D. Julius cum exercitu Britanniam ingreffus, quanquam profpera pugna terruerit incolas, ac litore potitus fit, poteft videri oftendiffe pofteris, non tradidiffe." Tacitus, Vit. Agric. c. xiii.

he effected, about the year of our Lord 43.*
Vespasian was the leader who chiefly signalised himself in the subjugation of Southern Britain. During his expedition into these parts, this successful commander, it is said, was victorious in thirty pitched battles; conquered two powerful nations; and planted the Roman standard in the Isle of Wight.†

It is probable this last acquisition was made without any great difficulty, since there are no vestiges of ancient camps or intrenchments, and very few *tumuli*,‡ that lead us to apprehend the inhabitants of the island struggled hard for the preservation of their liberties. It is indeed found, that constant commercial occupations have a tendency to destroy those finer sensibilities of the soul, without which, genuine patriotism, and a warm attachment to civil liberty, cannot

* "Divus Claudius, auctor operis, transvectis legionibus auxiliisque, et assumpto in partem rerum Vespasiano."
—Tacitus, ut supra.

† Tacitus, Hist. lib. III. cap. xliv.—Suetonius, in Vit. Vesp. cap. iv.

‡ These, by the bye, may be attributed to the times of the Danish descents.

subsist.

subsist. The merchants of the island, deeply engaged in the active pursuits of commerce, were altogether careless as to the *protection* under which it was carried on; whether it were the sanction of their own native laws, or the tolerating permission of a conqueror. While their traffic continued to be uninterrupted, and their accustomed gains to be received, they suffered but little concern from the idea of their most *sacred rights* being at the mercy of a foreign master. Justice, however, obliges us to confess, that the well-known lenity of the Romans to the nations which they reduced, justified, in a great degree, this confidence and unconcern on the part of the conquered. Their laws and their religion were generally uninfringed; their civil rights respected: or if any alteration were made in the one or the other, it was by the introduction of institutions that had a tendency to extend the comforts, and increase the happiness of life.*

* For a proof of this, advert to the conduct of Agricola, during his residence in Britain.—Tacitus, in Vit. Agric. c. xxi.

The

The Romans, having acquired the Isle of Wight, soon imposed the first badge of conquest upon it, by altering its name, which, by an easy variation, became *Vectis*, or *Vecta*, instead of *Ictis*. Tradition says, they also built a fortress on the site of Carisbrook, and formed it into a station; and, indeed, this is very likely to have been the case, since, in their selection of sites for these places of defence, they usually chose such spots as had been the ground-plots of British cities.* But the most material change which the Isle of Wight experienced, was the removal of the *tin-staple*, and the consequent declension of its trade. *Londinium*, or London, had now become the great emporium of the kingdom, and began to assume that consequence which it has ever since maintained. Hither the merchants of all nations flocked; and the first seeds of its present universal commerce might be seen, in the various articles its market exhibited,

* There is not, however, at present, the least trace of Roman architecture to be discerned.

exhibited, and the different people who crowded its exchange.*

But few traces of the Roman government have been difcovered in the Ifle of Wight, and thefe are confined to a fmall feries of coins, about ten or twelve in number, of fome of which the reader will find an account and engraving in the appendix.† They embrace, however, a confiderable period of time, and include fome of the emperors from Tiberius to Gal. Maximianus.

It is probable indeed, that a fmall number of the military were fufficient to preferve peace and order in this diftrict; and as the frontiers

---

* " Londinium———cognomento quidem coloniæ non infigne, fed copia negociatorum et commeatuum maxime celebre."—Tacitus, Annal. lib. XIV. c. xxxiii.

† Two coins are mentioned to have been found at Newport in 1759; one infcribed, TIBERIUS CÆSAR DIVI AUGUSTI FIL. AUGUSTUS.——Reverfe, PONTIFEX MAXIMUS. The other had, on one fide, a galley with a crofs at the ftern; and, on the reverfe, a cippus, furmounted by a globe crofs---a coin of the lower empire.—Gough's Camden, vol. I. p. 144.

of

of Wales, and North of Britain, required the prefence of all the legionaries that could be fpared, only a few foldiers would be left in the fortrefs of Carifbrook. This may account for the fcarcity of coins difcovered here; which are always found fomewhat abundantly in places where the Romans have been ftationary for any time.

If we take a view of the picture, that Vectis, and its inhabitants, would probably prefent, during the period of the Roman government there, we fhall not be aftonifhed at their being able to fupport their power in it, with the flight military force which they maintained.

It was invariably the plan of thefe mafters of the world, to bind the conquered nations to them, rather by the tie of *affection* than of *terror*; to treat them rather as *friends* than as *flaves*. Hence, the firft fteps they took, after having effectually fubdued them, was to introduce fuch arts, manufactures, and cuftoms among them, as would adminifter to their amufement as well as comfort. This conduct, indeed, might be

fuggefted

suggested rather by the *policy* of the Romans, than their humanity; since they were well aware, that modes of refinement, and habits of luxury, would more effectually enervate the mind, and extinguish that strong attachment to freedom, which burns so fiercely in the bosom of the hardy and unenlightened barbarian, than all the severities of slavery. This principle, then, they would of course adhere to, in their conduct to the inhabitants of the Isle of Wight. Such manufactures as were already in use among them, they would encourage and improve; such arts as were unknown to them, they would introduce and promote. The treasures of the soil whereon they lived, would be discovered and unfolded to them. The luxuries of life would be held up to their observation; and the bath and portico, the rich repast, and elegant attire, recommended to their use. Under these circumstances, their manners could be gradually refined into politeness; their minds illumined with science; and themselves, contented with the advantages which they possessed, utterly

for-

forgetful and regardlefs of the *high price* at which they were procured.

That this was the cafe in other parts of Britain, we know from the teftimony of an excellent hiftorian;* and that it was fo in the Ifle of Wight may be fairly inferred, from the peace and quietude of the diftrict, during the whole time the Romans poffeffed it; a fpace of four hundred years, wherein we read of no difturbances on the part of the conquered, nor of feverity on that of the victors.

* Tacitus. See his 'Life of Agricola;' wherein is depicted the refined policy of that commander, in thus foftening and fubduing the minds of the conquered Britons.

CHAP.

CHAP. III.

OF THE SAXONS, IN THE ISLE OF WIGHT.

THE peaceable, inactive state in which the Britons lived, during the continuance of the Romans among them, had, long before the departure of the latter to their own country, totally extinguished that enthusiastic love of liberty, that contempt of danger and death, which were striking features in the character of their ancestors, the ancient Britons. Debilitated by sensual indulgence, and effeminated by indolent voluptuousness, they were utterly inadequate, on the desertion of the Romans, to the protection of themselves against the tribes of barbarians, who, issuing from the mountains of Scotland, spread devastation and slaughter thro' all

all the Southern counties. Repeatedly did the unhappy Britons dispatch embassies to Rome, intreating the aid of their departed friends, who, equally pressed by the irruptions of barbarians, were obliged to concentrate their forces for the preservation of themselves. Assistance, however, was from time to time afforded them; till, at length the domestic necessities of the Romans not permitting them to impart further aid, they finally left the Britons to their own exertions, in the year of our Lord four hundred and forty-eight.*

The depredations of the Picts and Scots continually increasing, the Britons were reduced to the deepest distress; and, in the fatuity of despair, invited the Saxons, a warlike German people, to their assistance. A party of these freebooters, under their leaders, Hengist and Horsa, obeyed the summons, and landed from three vessels, about the year four hundred and forty-nine, in the Isle of Thanet.† They soon

* Bede, Eccl. Hist. lib. I. c. xiii. p. 55. Cantab. edit.
† Bede, lib. I. c. xv.

D   dispersed

dispersed the Northern depredators; but, observing the imbecility of the Britons, determined attempting the acquisition of a kingdom, which its inhabitants appeared unworthy to enjoy, and unable to defend. They soon put their determination into effect; and Hengist, after shedding oceans of blood, and committing the most horrible atrocities, seated himself on the throne of Kent, in the year of our Lord, four hundred and eighty-eight.*

* Bede, lib. I. c. xv. This venerable author, who lived at no great distance from these times, thus describes the devastations of the Saxons, and the deplorable state of the Britons. " Sic enim, et hic agente impio victore, imó disponente justo judice, proximas quasque civitates agrosque depopulans, (ab Orientali mari usque ad Occidentale,) nullo prohibente, suum continuavit incendium, totamque prope insulæ pereuntis superficiem oblexit. Ruebant ædificia publica, simul et privata; passim sacerdotes inter altaria trucidabantur; præsules, cum populis, sine ullo respectu honoris, ferro pariter ac flammis absumebantur: nec erat qui crudeliter interemptos sepulturæ traderet. Itaque nonnulli de miserandis reliquiis, in montibus comprehensi, acervatim jugulabantur. Alii fame confecti procedentes, manus hostibus dabant pro accipiendis alimentorum subsidiis; æternum subituri servitium, si tamen non continuó trucidarentur. Alii transmarinas regiones dolentes petebant."

Hitherto

Hitherto the Isle of Wight, lying rather remote from the scene of action, had not been agitated by the convulsions which tore the South-Eastern parts of the kingdom; but the period of its suffering similar evils was approaching. In the year four hundred and ninety-five, Cerdic, and his son Cinric, at the head of a large band of Germans, who chiefly consisted of a race of people called *Jutes*,* landed in England, excited to action by the success which had crowned the arms of his Saxon brethren here. Though their irruptions were opposed by the unconquerable spirit of Arthur, the gallant prince of the Silures; yet, aided by continual supplies from the continent, and the assistance of such tribes as had already gained a footing in England, they at length bore down all opposition, and in the year five hundred and thirty gained possession of the Isle of Wight.†

* Saxon Chronicle, p. 12. Bede, lib. I. c. xv. "De Jutarum origine sunt Cantuarii et *Vectuarii*, hoc est, ea gens quæ *Vectam tenet insulam.*"

† Sax. Chron. edit. Cantab. Wheloc. p. 509.

A spirit

A spirit of revenge is one of the most striking features of the savage character; and hence it is that, in all the contests of barbarous nations, the scene of blood is seldom closed, without the infliction of death or torture on the persons of the conquered. Irritated by opposition, the two Saxon leaders followed the dictates of unbridled passion, and slew most of the inhabitants whom the rage of war had spared, in cold blood, at the city of Carisbrook.* Cerdic, the first Saxon monarch of the Isle of Wight, died, A. D. 534; and bequeathed this acquisition to his nephew Withgar,† or, according to some authors, to his two nephews, Withgar and Stuffa.‡

* Bede, ut supra. "Cirtic namque, et Cinric filius ejus, congregatis ingentibus copiis apud Withland, præliati sunt, belloque devictam insulam cepêrunt, et innumerabilem hostium stragem fecêrunt apud Witgaresbrige xiii anno regni sui."—Leland, Collect. vol. II. p. 293.

† "Cerdic moriens dedit Vectam insulam Withgaro suo ex sorore nepoti, qui postea eâdem regnavit."—Leland, Collect. vol. I. p. 78.

‡ Sax. Chron. p. 18.

These

These ferocious chieftains filled up the measure of woes which the unhappy Britons of the Island were doomed to experience; and actually murdered all such of them as had survived the persecutions of their uncle *Cerdic*.* Withgar also gave a new appellation to Carisbrook, its most considerable town; which was now called, after his own name, *Withgarisburg*, that is, the city of Withgar. †

Thus have we seen the Isle of Wight change its inhabitants a second time. The Saxons now possessed it entirely, and, though sometimes disturbed by the transient visits of the Danes, retained the undivided possession of it for five centuries, till the conquest of the kingdom by the Normans.

We find nothing recorded relative to this district, from the massacre by Withgar to the year six hundred and sixty-one, when it was attacked and laid waste by Wulpher King of

* Sax. Chron. p. 18.

† The island itself also began to be called Wiht, or Wihtland—an easy corruption of the Roman Vecta, or Vectis.

Mercia,

Mercia, the fon of Penda. He prefented his conqueft to Edelwalch, King of the South Saxons, who had been his baptifmal fponfor.* The Ifle of Wight continued fubject to this monarch till the year fix hundred and eighty-fix, when Ceadwalla, a lineal defcendant of Cerdic, and King of Weffex, flew Adelwalch, and annexed this territory to his own dominions. As the iflanders were yet idolaters, this warrior, in the true fpirit of the times, determined to exterminate the whole of them, and people their habitations with his own fubjects. A fourth part of thefe devoted wretches were, however, faved, in confequence of a vow which he had made, when attempting to conquer the ifland, of dedicating this proportion of its inhabitants, and their lands, to the Lord. He performed this vow by conferring three hundred families (for the ifland only contained twelve hundred), and their property, on Bifhop *Wilfred*; who committed the care of them, and the diftrict, to a nephew of his own, a prieft called Bernwinus.†

* Sax. Chron. Wheloc. p. 516.
† Bede, lib. IV. c. xvi.

This

This anecdote is fomewhat curious, as it gives us an opportunity of comparing the population of the ifland eleven hundred years ago, with the ftate of it at prefent; for if we allow an average of five fouls to a family, we fhall find that it contained, in the feventh century, not more than fix thoufand inhabitants; whereas a conjectural cenfus, made about four years ago, brought its population to eighteen thoufand feven hundred fouls. A prodigious increafe; and a ftriking example of what agriculture and commerce are gradually able to effect.

The Ifle of Wight prefents but a gloomy and difgufting appearance during the early periods of the Saxon dominion in it. Every veftige of refinement difappeared when the Britons were exterminated. Their conquerors, remarkable only for determined valor and the boundlefs love of freedom, neither refpected, nor cultivated, the arts of peace. Commerce and hufbandry were alike neglected; war and hunting alone purfued; and a cloud of ignorance, ferocity, and fuperftition, fettled for centuries over the whole diftrict.

CHAP.

CHAP. IV.

OF THE DANES, AND NORMANS, IN THE ISLE OF WIGHT.

THE Saxons did not long retain the undisturbed possession of the Isle of Wight. A formidable enemy, towards the latter part of the ninth century, began to interrupt their quiet. This was the *Danes*, a ferocious race, who inhabited Denmark, Sweden, Jutland, and the other frozen regions of the North. The penury of their own country had early impelled these people to commit depredations on happier climes; and in consequence of these freebooting habits they had acquired considerable skill in naval tactics. Their ships, being small and light, were easily managed, and extremely swift. With these they ran up rivers and creeks; hauled

hauled them afhore; raifed a flight rampart around them; and then began the work of plunder. Having effected as much havoc as they could; and collected as much booty as they were able to carry away, they immediately embarked; and, before meafures could be taken to repel them, were at fea.

These ravagers had made feveral defcents on the Southern coaft, before they attempted the Ifle of Wight.* At length fix Danifh fhips, in the year eight hundred and ninety-feven, appeared off this place; the crews of which, landing, committed great depredations, and then failed for the coaft of Devonfhire. The throne of England, was, however, at this time filled by a prince altogether equal to the arduous times in which he lived. *Alfred*, ever attentive to the aggrandizement of his country, and the improvement of his fubjects, had obferved the fuperiority of the Danifh to the Englifh fhips, and had already conftructed veffels higher, longer, and fwifter, than thofe of his enemies. Nine of

* Sax. Chron. p. 64 et 73.

this defcription he difpatched to the Weft of England, to intercept and punifh the Northern invaders. Thefe effectually revenged the outrages which had been committed, by taking two of the Danifh fhips; driving three on fhore; and killing a great number of their men. Such as were taken prifoners, Alfred tried as pirates at Winchefter, and condemned them to be hanged.*

To particularize the various tranfient vifits of thefe naval robbers to the Ifle of Wight, would be tirefome and ufelefs; as they were attended with no permanent effect, and as they all exhibit the fame difgufting fcene of unmerciful butchery and wafting conflagration. We pafs over, therefore, the temporary diftreffes of the iflanders, occafioned by thefe inroads; as well as the defcent of Earl Godwin, in the year one thoufand and fifty-two,† (who had been outlawed by Edward the Confeffor,) and the invafion of Tofti, fon of Earl Godwin, in one

* Sax. Chron. Wheloc, p. 546.
† Sax. Chron. p. 166.

thoufand

thoufand and fixty-fix; * that we may notice the more weighty alterations which took place in the internal ftate of the ifland by the Norman conqueft.

The important battle of *Haftings*, fought on the fourteenth day of October, in the year of our Lord one thoufand and fixty-fix, put the crown of England, together with the dominion of the Ifle of Wight, and other dependancies, into the poffeffion of William the Norman.

It is obferved, that what is acquired with eafe, is, generally, diffipated with thoughtleffnefs; an axiom, the truth of which is well exemplified in the extravagant munificence with which the Conqueror rewarded the barons who attended him in this expedition. His kinfman, William Fitz-Ofborne, ftood particularly high in his favor; as he had long been a confidential friend; had planned and affifted the attempt on England; been marfhal of the Norman army at the battle of Haftings, and, by his active valor, had greatly contributed to the fuccefs of that well-fought

* Florence of Worcefter, p. 428. edit. 1592.

day,

day. These services the monarch rewarded by the donation of the Isle of Wight; to be held by Fitz-Osborne, as freely as William himself held the realm of England.* The Norman baron imitated the bounty of his lord, and distributed the lands, thus conferred on him, among the sub-feudatories who ranged themselves under his standard. What became, in the mean time, of the unfortunate inhabitants of the island, thus bereft of all their property, we are not informed; but it is likely many of them perished through want, as was the case in several parts of the kingdom; while others were content to lengthen a wretched existence by becoming slaves, on those lands which they had formerly held as their own.

William Fitz-Osborne, first lord of the Isle of Wight, enjoyed his acquisition only four years, being slain in battle on the continent. He was succeeded in his dignity by Roger de Breteville, Earl of Hereford, his third son.

* Chartulary of Carisbrook priory, in the possession of Sir Richard Worsley, bart.

Gratitude

Gratitude is so much the virtue of a cultivated mind, that it is but rarely found among the illiterate and unenlightened. Of this description was the Earl of Hereford, who, unmindful of the obligations which William had conferred on his family, and the personal favors he himself had received at his hands, entered into a conspiracy to depose him, during his absence in Normandy. Waltheof, Earl of Northumberland, however, one of the conspirators, disclosed the secret, which gave William an opportunity of checking it in the bud. Earl Roger was taken, tried, found guilty, and condemned to perpetual imprisonment. His lands were confiscated, and the Isle of Wight, amongst the rest, escheated to the crown.*

This valuable lordship was a second time bestowed on a subject, during the reign of Henry the first, who granted it to Richard de Redvers, a Norman of high descent. On his death, which occurred in the year one thousand one hundred and thirty-five, Baldwin de Redvers, his son, succeeded to the dignity. Being a

* Dugdale's Baron, vol. I. p. 67.

devoted

devoted partizan of the emprefs Maud, he was one of the firſt to rebel againſt the uſurped authority of Stephen. He therefore fortified his caſtle of Exeter, put the Iſle of Wight in a ſtate of defence, and boldly defied the king. Stephen, however, proved too powerful for him; his fortreſs was taken; the iſland ſubdued; and himſelf obliged to fly the kingdom:* Shortly after this event, an accommodation took place between the contending parties, when the honors and poſſeſſions, which Baldwin had loſt in the ſtruggle, were again reſtored to him; and he had an opportunity of bequeathing the lordſhip of the Iſle of Wight to his ſon Richard, in the year one thouſand one hundred and fifty-four.†

After paſſing lineally through ſeveral of the Redvers family, the Iſle of Wight devolved to

* Annalı Waverly, p. 154.

† In the year one thouſand one hundred and ſeventy-ſeven, during the time the iſland was in the poſſeſſion of Baldwin's nephew, Richard, a fearful miracle is ſaid to have happened in it; a *ſhower of blood* of two hours continuance. " Pluit in inſulâ Vectæ xiii. cal. ſanguineus imber, fere per duas horas integras."—Lel. Col. vol. I. p. 326.

William

William de Vernon, a collateral branch of the fame ſtock, anno domini one thouſand one hundred and eighty-four. The oppreſſive gripe of King John was extended to this nobleman, out of whom he ſqueezed a fine of five hundred marks, on reinſtating him in his caſtle of Plympton, and allowing him to govern his Iſle of Wight tenants, by military ſervice, and, according to the laws of the land, by judgment in his court.*

It was by this, and ſimilar acts of harſhneſs and injuſtice towards his barons, that John at length rouſed the ſpirit of this formidable claſs of his ſubjects; who, rather for the purpoſe of re-dreſſing their own wrongs, than emancipating the great body of the people from the oppreſſions under which they groaned, raiſed the ſtandard of rebellion, and obliged the tyrant to ſign that great charter which is the ſacred foundation and bulwark of all our liberties.

It has been obſerved, however, by an hiſtorian, on an occaſion analogous to this, that "the king

* Sir Richard Worſley's Hiſt. p. 54.

meant

meant not to bind himself with fetters of parchment;" a remark extremely applicable to the ratification of *Magna Charta*: for as soon as John had pacified the furious barons, by complying with their demands, he resolved not to rest, till he again released himself from the obligations which necessity and fear had imposed upon him. Scarcely therefore had the assertors of freedom retired to their respective castles, when the king applied to the pope for absolution from the tremendous oaths by which he had ratified the great charter. He also empowered his favorites to raise bodies of mercenary soldiers, in Germany, France, and Flanders, to assist his meditated revenge on the barons, and his encroachments on the budding liberties of his subjects. During the time these crafty negociations were on foot, the king retired into the Isle of Wight, that he might be less exposed to the observation of the public. Here he continued some time, confining himself to the society of the lower ranks of people, such as fishermen and sailors; a conduct which raised

the

the curiofity of all, and the merriment of many, who afferted he had turned fifherman, or merchant; or intended to betake himfelf to the profeffion of piracy.*

It is fomewhat odd, indeed, the monarch fhould choofe this fpot for the place of his concealment; fince it was then in the poffeffion of William de Vernon, a baron who had been extremely active in his oppofition to him. Perhaps, however, as the ratification of Magna Charta had produced a kind of fpecious reconciliation between John and his nobility, he apprehended he might remain with tolerable fafety on the demefne of De Vernon, till his plans were fufficiently matured; aware that the fecrecy of his negociations would preclude a difcovery of the intentions he harboured, and the real manner in which he was employed.

The Ifle of Wight defcended, through Baldwin the grandfon, and Baldwin the great-grandfon, of William de Vernon, to Ifabella, (the daughter of the latter Baldwin,) who obtained

* Rapin's Hift. Eng. vol. I. p. 277.

poffeffion of its lordfhip in the twelfth year of Edward I. This lady married William de Fortibus, Earl of Albemarle, and, furviving him, was ftyled Countefs of Albemarle, and Lady of the Ifle of Wight. In the thirteenth century, and for fome centuries afterwards, it was cuftomary for the great barons to refide upon their eftates, begirt by numerous dependants and retainers, and furrounded with the barbaric magnificence of the age. The Countefs Ifabella, on the deceafe of her lord, chofe Carifbrook caftle for the place of her abode, where fhe lived for fome years in almoft regal fplendor; adminiftering juftice; difpenfing charity; and heaping donations (according to the miftaken piety of the times) on the numerous monafteries under her protection.

Upon her death-bed, it appears fhe was prevailed upon by the agents of Edward I. to alienate to the crown this valuable lordfhip, for the fum of fix thoufand marks. Walter, Bifhop of Litchfield and Coventry, drew the deed of fale; which was executed by the countefs,

tefs, a few hours before her death, in the year 1293 :* not without ſtrong fufpicions of improper advantages having been taken of the weaknefs and fatuity which generally precede the hour of diffolution.†

* Rot. Parl. 8 et 9, Edward II.

† Dugdale, Baron. vol. I, p. 55 et 56. The fmallnefs of the purchafe-money, and other circumſtances, feem to indicate fomething fraudulent and difhonorable in this tranfaction; fince fix thoufand marks (about £4000 ſterling) can never, by any reafonable mode of calculating the comparative value of money, be fuppofed to have been the real worth of the iſland in the thirteenth century. Befides, Edward himſelf, a few years previous to Ifabella's death, had entered into a treaty with her daughter Aveline, and Edmund Crouchback her huſband, to pay her no leſs than twenty thoufand marks, together with the grant of an eſtate, for a fimple aſſurance of this valuable lordſhip, to himſelf and heirs, after the deceaſe of her mother; a treaty which was annulled by the premature death of Aveline. Gough's Camden, vol. I. p. 125.

CHAP.

CHAP. V.

MILITARY HISTORY OF THE ISLAND, FROM EDWARD THE FIRST TO THE PRESENT TIME.

DURING the time the Isle of Wight continued in the De Redvers family, its poffeffors feem to have held it by the moft free and independent tenure. By the grant of Henry I. to Richard de Redvers, that baron became poffeffed not only of the royal demefnes within this diftrict, but was invefted alfo with the dominion of the whole ifland; holding it under

the

the crown in efcuage,* at fifteen knights' fees and an half.†

A fief of fuch importance, of confiderable magnitude, and great ſtrength from the circumſtances of its fituation, was foon found, in the turbulent and unfettled ſtate of the government at this period, to give too much confequence to a fubjeƈt, and afford him too frequent opportunities of infulting and endangering regal authority. The wifdom of Edward I., therefore, determined him to make the Ifle of Wight an appendage to the crown, and his policy at length gave him poſſeſſion of it, in the manner mentioned in the laſt chapter.

* According to the cuſtoms of the feudal fyſtem, the king could demand the perfonal attendance of all his vaſſals in war. This troublefome fervice was, however, very foon changed into a pecuniary compofition, which was aptly enough termed *efcuage*, from the word *fcutum*, the Latin for fhield. It was a fum paid upon every knight's fee, for fome reigns precarious and uncertain; being at times 20s. per knight's fee, at others, 2 marks, &c.

† One knight's fee was compofed of four hydes of land; and each hyde contained one hundred *Norman acres*, which were equal to one hundred and twenty *Engliſh* ones. Arthur Agarde, p. 9.

Shortly

Shortly after Edward's purchase of it, the preparations of Philip, King of France, to invade the English coast, threw the Southern part of the kingdom into some consternation; and a descent being apprehended on the Isle of Wight, Edward took proper precautions for its defence, by giving a joint commission to the Bishop of Winchester, Adam de Gordon,* and Sir Richard de Affeton, to act as wardens of it. The French force, however, took a direction more to the

* This Adam de Gordon was a famous rebel and freebooter in the reign of Henry III., who ranged through the extensive forests of Hampshire, committing depredations on all who fell into his hands. He became at length sufficiently formidable to merit the notice of government, and Prince Edward was dispatched in pursuit of him. They met near Alton in Hampshire, and a desperate single combat immediately commenced between them; in which Edward was at length victorious, though not without great difficulty. Instead of being enraged by the opposition of Gordon, the young prince was struck with admiration of his valor; pardoned him on the spot for his former atrocities, and received him into his confidence and friendship. A curious example of the romantic spirit of the times; and a remarkable instance of generous gallantry in Edward. T. Wikes, p. 76.

Eastward;

Eaftward, attacked the town of Dover, reduced it to afhes, and retired.*

The peace of the ifland continued unmolefted till the reign of Edward III.; whofe abfurd claims to the crown of France involved him in a war with France, which, though brilliant with refpect to temporary fuccefs, was extremely pernicious to his country in its confequences. During thefe hoftilities, the Ifle of Wight was repeatedly threatened with a defcent, which induced the iflanders to enter into regulations for their fecurity, of the following nature : †

1. That there fhould be but three ports in the ifland; namely, La Riche, Shamblord, and Yarmouth.

2. That three perfons fhould be appointed wardens of thefe ports, who were to prevent any one from retiring from the ifland, or exporting provifions from thence without licence.

3. That none but licenfed boats fhould be permitted to pafs, except the boat belonging to

* Trivetus, p. 284.
† Rot. Par. 12th Edward III.

the

the abbot of Quar; a boat belonging to Sir Bartholomew de Lifle, and another belonging to Robert de Pimely.

4. That feveral watches fhould be appointed, and perfons nominated to fuperintend them and the beacons.*

Nor were thefe precautions ufelefs, for in the thirteenth of Edward III., the French actually landed at the Eaftern extremity of the ifland, in confiderable force. They were, however, foon oppofed by Sir John de Longford, Sir Bartholomew de Lifle, and Sir Theobald Ruffel, (who had been appointed wardens,) with a body of iflanders under their command. A fharp conflict enfued, in which Sir Theobald Ruffell was flain, but the French were obliged to retire with lofs to their fhipping.

The fituation of the ifland, immediately oppofite to the coaft of France, rendered it always liable to vifits from the French, before the exiftence of thofe caftles, which the prudence of Henry VIII. erected. So that there was fcarcely

* Sir R. Worfley, p. 31.

a war

a war with that kingdom from the thirteenth to the seventeenth century, in which some attempts were not made to land in the Isle of Wight. Many of the inhabitants, indeed, conscious of its exposed situation, and the constant danger in which they stood of losing their lives and fortunes, during the almost perpetual hostilities between France and England in the fourteenth century, voluntarily withdrew, with their effects, to the coast of Hampshire: and this spirit of emigration began to be so universal amongst them, that Edward III. was obliged to enforce their continuance on it, by an order to the wardens, that the lands of those who had retired from the island, and did not immediately return, should be seized, and escheat to the crown.*

It appears

* Brev. Regis de Morando in Inf. Vectâ, 51. Ed. III. Rex dilectis et fidel. suis, Johi. de Cavendish et sociis suis justiciariis ad placita coram nobis tenenda assignatis, sal., &c. Cum insula Vecta, quæ infra littus maris in comitatu Southamptoniæ situatur, hostibus nostris publicis maximè sit propinqua, quam etiam insulam iidem hostes multùm desiderant; et cum, infra breve tempus, appropinquare et debellare proponunt, ut. audivimus, et se parant. Nos licet de avisamento concilii nostri sessiones nostras

It appears that their apprehensions were not without foundation. Early in Richard's reign, the French, with a multitude of gallies and ships, landed at the village of Rye, which they burnt to the ground, making prisoners of many of its inhabitants, and murdering the rest. They then proceeded into the heart of the island, and attacked Carisbrook-castle, whither numbers of the islanders had retired for protection. This fortress was defended by a gallant knight, Sir Hugh Tyrrel, who, by his prudence and bravery, at length obliged the invaders to retire, but not before they had extorted a contribution of one thousand marks from the inhabitants, who were

---

nostras in com. prædicto ad placita coram nobis tenenda quamdiu nostræ placuerit voluntati ordinaverimus, volumus tamen et jubemus quod omnes et singuli residentes et habitantes in insula Vectâ, cujuscunque fuerint statûs et conditionis, salvationi et defensioni ejusdem insulæ continué intendant, et ibidem moram faciant et remaneant, absque eo quod ipsi seu eorum aliquis coram nobis in sessionibus nostris in comitatu prædicto comparere seu venire, vel in assisis juratis seu recognitionibus aliquibus ibidem (quanquam nos specialiter tangant,) poni seu panellari non compellatur, aut tenentur quocunque modo vel colore quousque aliud inde duxerimus demandandum, &c. Rymer's Fœd. vol. VII. p. 147.

glad-

glad, by these means, to rescue their houses and property from fire and devastation.*

The annalists have transmitted to us some other accounts of attempts by the French to surprise this place. One of these occurred in the fifth year of Henry V., when a large party of them landed, for the purpose, as they asserted, of *keeping Christmas there*: their entertainment, however, was but a sorry one; for the islanders being apprized of their arrival, suddenly attacked, and destroyed, a great number of them.

Not learning prudence from their ill success, they made another hostile visit a short time after this failure, demanding a subsidy, in the name of Richard II. and Isabella his queen. The conduct of the islanders on the occasion, marks

* In this expedition the French burned the towns of Newtown and Yarmouth. They made the following stipulation also with the inhabitants, before they agreed to retire, which is ridiculous enough, from the improbability of its being regarded, had the invaders insisted on its observance;. That, should they return within twelve months after their departure, *the islanders would not attempt to interrupt their devastations.*

strongly

strongly the spirit of the times; and gives us very favorable impressions of their courage and generosity. They denied any money being due from them to the French; but added, if the latter had any inclination to try their prowess in battle, they should land without molestation, and be allowed six hours to rest and refresh themselves; after which interval, the men of the island would meet them in fair combat. The invitation was declined, however, on the part of the French, and they speedily decamped.

Henry VIII. was the first of our monarchs who adopted the plan of building forts on those parts of the British coasts which were most exposed to the insults of the French. He erected several along the shores of the Isle of Wight. Perhaps he was induced to this by some descents made by that people during his wars with Francis I., whose marine seems to have been more numerous than his own. In the thirty-sixth year of his reign, Annebout, the French admiral, landed two thousand men in three different parts of the island, with an intention to take possession of, of, and fortify it for his master, the King of France. But a council of war having determined the impracticability of this scheme, the invaders contented themselves with burning and laying waste the villages; in which work they were busily employed, when Richard Worsley, Captain of the Island, attacked, and drove them to their ships, with the loss of the admiral, and a great part of his forces.

The powerful naval preparations of Spain against England, stimulated Elizabeth to bend her particular attention towards the increase of the British Marine. Her exertions were such, that she soon put it upon a footing sufficiently respectable to brave the power of Philip, and to gain that ascendency which her successors have ever since maintained. Her navies were found to be a surer defence against the attempts of foreign enemies, than all the fortresses which her father had erected; and the neighbourhood of Portsmouth, that now became the rendezvous of ships of war, gave additional security to the Isle of Wight, which, from this time, does not

appear

appear to have suffered farther by French invasions.

Early in the civil wars of the laft century, the Parliament became poffeffed of the Ifle of Wight, by the removal of Jerom, Earl of Portland, (who was attached to the caufe of the ill-fated Charles,) from the government of it. This nobleman had rendered himfelf extremely popular, during the exercife of his authority, by the affability of his manners, and his generous hofpitality. Infomuch that, when the Parliament fuddenly imprifoned him, upon the abfurd pretences of his being a favorer of popery, and a thoughtlefs expender of the ammunition entrufted to his care, the chief inhabitants of the ifland drew up and prefented the following petition to the parliament in his behalf.

" To the honourable the knights, citizens, and burgeffes, of the houfe of commons, affembled in parliament;"

" The humble petition of the deputy-lieutenants and juftices of the peace, the mayors and corporations of Newport, Newtown, and
Yarmouth;

Yarmouth; and of the reſt of the inhabitants of the Iſle of Wight."

" Preſenting to your gracious conſideration our generall griefe for the queſtioning of Jerom, Earl of Portland, our noble and much honoured and beloved captayne and governor."

" The principal imputation, as we are given to underſtand, being a jealouſy of his lordſhip's inclination to popery."

" For ourſelves, we have a pregnant teſtimony amongſt us of his pious affection and love to the reformed religion, by a conſtant weekly lecture at Newport, to which his lordſhip is a principal benefactor. So are there on the other ſide, ſo ſmall effects to be ſeen, of his lordſhip's diſcourſe or practiſe that way tending, that amongſt all the inhabitants of this iſle, we have not one profeſſed papiſt, or, to our knowledge, popiſhly affected; ſo rare a bleſſing, in theſe times, as we ſuppoſe cannot be boaſted in any tract of ground, of this extent, in all the kingdom of England."

" Some other weake aſperſions uppon his lordſhip, we thought not worthy of our owne regard,

regard, much leffe dare, wee prefume to remember them to fo grave and wife a fenate; wee do therefore, at once, with this petition, prefent our humble and gratefull acknowledgment to this greate and good affembly, of the care that is taken of our weale and fafety, which wee conceive can no waye be better advanced and continued uppon us, than by your juft approbation of the vigilance and fidelity of our prudent and able governor."*

The above reprefentation being difregarded by the parliament, the moft refpeɛtable gentlemen of the ifland feemed inclined to enforce a compliance with what they had, in vain, requefted; and aɛtually entered into a fpirited declaration againft the proceedings of the houfe of commons, ftating, that it was their determination to fupport, with their lives and fortunes, the proteftant religion, " and admit no forreyn power or forces, or new government; except his majefty, by advice of his parliament, uppon occafione that may arife, fhall think itt neceffary to alter it in

* Sir R. Worfley's Hift. p. 110.

any

any particulars, for the good and safety of the kingdom;" this was subscribed with twenty-four names.*

Notwithstanding, however, the inclination of the Isle of Wight *gentry*, to befriend the cause of the unfortunate Charles, the populace, whose affections are as uncertain as worthless, instigated by the seditious spirit of Moses Read, Mayor of Newport, declared in favor of the parliament; and a representation was transmitted to this assembly, of great danger accruing to the state, from the Countess of Portland being allowed to continue in Carisbrooke castle, and Col. Brett retaining the custody of it. In consequence of this, orders were sent to Read, to seize immediately on this fortress; and to secure the temporary governor, and the Earl of Portland's lady, together with her five children, and other relatives, who had sheltered themselves in it. The rebel mayor marched, therefore, with the Newport Militia, and a body of four hundred

* Sir R. Worsley, p. 115: the declaration bears date, August 8th, 1642.

sailors, to attack the garrison of Carisbrooke, which, at that time, did not consist of more than twenty men. We blush for the degeneracy of our kind, when we relate, that Harby, the curate of Newport, who was bound to the Earl of Portland by the strongest ties of gratitude, prostituted his sacred office, by exhorting, from the pulpit, this rebellious band, to sweep from the earth the unfortunate Countess, with her innocent offspring.

This lady, however, animated by that unbending fortitude which springs from conscious rectitude, was no ways distressed at the prodigious disproportion between the numbers of her assailants and defenders. She knew it was impossible for her little garrison long to resist the enemy's attacks, but, at the same time, was determined not to surrender it, without assurance of receiving the most honorable terms of capitulation. She roused the spirits of the desponding soldiers, by her animating exhortations; and added the force of example to the persuasion of eloquence. With a lighted match in her hand, she

she walked deliberately to one of the bastions, declaring she would discharge the first cannon at the foe. Read, and his party, unwilling perhaps to provoke the dangerous efforts of despair, offered terms of capitulation, which, after some negociations, were accepted, and the castle was surrendered on the following stipulations; That the warder of the castle, Col. Brett, together with his servants, and the garrison, should be allowed the freedom of the island, under the restriction of their forbearing to visit Portsmouth, which Goring at that time held for Charles. That the countess, with her family and friends, should be allowed to continue her residence in the castle, till such time as the parliament had declared its pleasure in that respect. Her stay here was not long protracted; the house of commons, with invidious expedition, immediately transmitted an order for her to remove from the island, within two days after the receipt of it. Yet such was the height to which the spirit of fanaticism had already arisen, in this part of England, that not a single islander could be

found,

found, who would undertake to convey to the oppofite fhore, one, whofe confort had been fufpected of favoring popery; and it is probable the unfortunate countefs might have been *compelled* to neglect the orders of the council, had not the feamen of a trading veffel, with that generous compaffion which characterizes the maritime profeffion, taken her and her family on board their fhip, and conveyed them fafely to the coaft of Hampfhire.

From this period, the hiftory of the Ifle of Wight ceafes to afford further military anecdote. On the Earl of Pembroke fucceeding Col. Brett, its inhabitants quietly funk under the control of the parliament; and witneffed, without an effort to prevent it, the unnatural imprifonment of their anointed fovereign, in Carifbrook caftle, and the forcible abduction of him from thence to the fcaffold at Whitehall. On the reftoration of his fon, they as patiently and willingly received the governor appointed by the court, Thomas, Lord Culpeper; and, during the whole troublefome period of the civil war, occupied entirely

by

by their agricultural and commercial purfuits, kept the " noifelefs tenor of their way;" without being involved in thofe convulfions, which fhook the peace of almoft every other part of the kingdom.*

* " The quiet they enjoyed invited many from the neighbouring counties to retire hither; which raifed the rents of the farms in the proportion of twenty pounds in the hundred. That the rife originated from this caufe only, appeared by their finking again, foon after the Reftoration."—Sir R. Worfley's Hift. Ifle of Wight, p. 136.

CHAP.

CHAP. VI.

THE ANCIENT AND PRESENT DEFENCE OF THE ISLE OF WIGHT.

DURING the continuance of the Roman government in Britain, the univerſal empire of that people precluded the neceſſity of keeping a military force in the iſland, to defend it from external attacks. The few legionaries who dwelt in the ſtation at Cariſbrook, were placed there for the purpoſe of preſerving internal peace and order; which, from the cauſes mentioned in a preceding chapter, were eaſily maintained throughout the diſtrict. Not but that the iſlanders had it in their power to be troubleſome to their conquerors, provided their inclination had been ſuch; for although Claudius, on his ſubduing the Southern parts of Britain, deprived,

for

for a time, its inhabitants of their arms; yet thefe were again reftored, as foon as their minds were reconciled to the dominion of the Roman power.*

The excellent regulations of Alfred, with whom originated the idea of a national militia, † enabled the Ifle of Wight to repel the repeated defcents of the Danes; nor could they effect any ferious impreffions on it, fo long as thofe regulations were properly obferved.

From the time that William Fitz-Ofborne received the abfolute dominion of the Ifle of Wight, the defence of it refted entirely with itfelf. Being totally diftinct from the crown, it was not to expect the interference of that power, in cafe of foreign affaults. But the feudal fyftem provided ample refources for its protection. According to the fpirit of this mingled mafs of wifdom and abfurdity, each land-holder was a foldier; and bound to attend the lord of the fee in his wars. A principle that certainly

* Dio. p. 959.
† Afferius de Vit. Ælfredi, p. 6.

was

was not without its advantages, whilft ftrictly adhered to; fince it furnifhed, on every emergency, a band of warriors who were bound by the ftrong tie of *intereft*, as well as the facred obligation of oaths, to exert every effort in the field of battle.

Although Richard de Redvers did not receive the Ifle of Wight on fuch independent and unfettered terms, as William Fitz-Ofborne had it from the Norman on; yet, with refpect to its defence, he alone was to provide the means of that. And we find, accordingly, that fo long as it continued in his family, a fupply of seventy-fix men at arms was always drawn from Devonfhire, (of which county the Redvers family were earls,) whenever the profpect of external hoftility rendered fuch fuccour neceffary for the iflanders.*

As foon, however, as Edward I. was poffeffed of it, the means of its fecurity became of courfe the care of the crown. The following lift of men at arms, furnifhed to this monarch, for its defence,

* Inq. Ann. 16mo Ed. III.

will

HISTORY OF THE ISLE OF WIGHT. 57

will difplay the nature and the fources of its protection at this time:

	MEN.
From the Bifhop of Salifbury	5
From the Abbot of Glaftonbury	7
From John Mandut	1
From Emmeline Longefpey	1
From the Abbot of Stanley	2
From Beatrice de Winterfhall	1
From the Abbot of Gloucefter	1
From the Abbefs of Godeflow	1
From Robert de Keynis	1
From the Abbot of Malmfbury	3
From the Abbot of Cirencefter	2
From Thomas Warblington	1
From the Prior of Hurle	1
From Thomas de Ambrofbury	1
From the Abbot of Abyngdon	3
From Elia Molendinari	1
From John Dandele	1
From William Pagham	1
From Richard Winton	1
From Peter Coudray	1
From Hugh Taylor	1
From the Abbot of Romele	1
From Lucia de Grey	1

From

	MEN.
From the Abbot of Walton	1
From the Preceptor of Shalford	1
From the Preceptor of Conele	1
From Nicholas Burden	1
From Roger de St. Martin	1
From Mary the king's daughter, a nun at Ambresbury	2
From the Bishop of Worcester	1
From Hamon de Parles	1
From the Bishop of Bath and Wells	1
From Robert Kingborne, for William de Coates	1
John Grey, for Walter Skydemour	1
John Blaine, for the Abbot of Thukesburgh	1
Richard Selby, for the Hundred of Herewalkeden	1
Henry Hemenhall, for Chipham and Malmsbury	1
Walter Cornisey, for the Hundred of Warham	1
John Carrile, for Chalk and Domerham	1
Geoffry de Calne, for Heightsbury	1
From Roger de Coke, for Westbury	1
From the Abbess of Whorwell	1
From Hugh Peverell	1
From William Ires, for the Abb. of Shafton	1
From Maurice de Wileb, for Matthew Fitz John	1
From —— Sterne	1
From the Community of Wilts	6
From Alife de Bavent	1

From

		MEN.
From the Prior of ———	- - -	1
From Adam de Breton	- - -	1
*From Richard de la Rivere	- - -	1
In all—Men at Arms	- - -	73

Exclusive of this band of auxiliaries, every free land-holder, to the amount of twenty pounds per annum, was obligated by his tenure to find one horseman, completely armed and accoutred, at his own proper charges, in all times of actual danger. It appears also, that for the better security of the island against surprizes, various beacons and watches were established in different parts, at which constant duty was performed both night and day. Of these there were thirteen in the Eastern division of the island, and sixteen in the Western division; and each of them, (for the most part) had four men to watch at it during the night, and two by day.† To these means

of

* Prynne on the 4th Institute, p. 211.

† Inquisitio anno 18. Edw. II. num. 216. in Tur. Lond. N. B. The island, from very early antiquity

of defence were added one hundred flingers and bowmen sent by the king, and three hundred by the city of London.*

Early in the reign of Edward III. we find the number of forces furnished by the land-holders of the island, amounted to fifty-four men at arms, and one hundred and forty-two bowmen, who were produced by the persons, and in the proportions which follow:

	ARM.	SAG.
The Abbot of Quarr	4	0
The Lord of Woodyton	6	0
The Abbefs (of Laycock) for Sherwell	3	2
The Prior of Chriftchurch	2	2
The Lord of Yaverland	2	2
The Lord of Apuldurcomb	2	2
The Lord of Kingfton	1	0
The Lord of Wonfton	1	0

quity, has been divided into two Hundreds, called Eaft and Weft Medine.—They receive thefe names from their relative fituations to the river *Medina*, which like moft other of our rivers, has preferved its Britifh appellation; *Med* in the Celtic fignifying water, and *in* being the Britifh plural.

* Inquif. 16. anno Ed. III. in Tur. Lond.

The

HISTORY OF THE ISLE OF WIGHT. 61

	ARM.	SAG.
The Lord of Standen and Wode	1	0
The Manor of Whitefield	1	0
The Manor of Stenbury	1	0
The Lord of Niton and Chale	0	1
The Manor of Bottebridge	0	1
The Prior of St. Helens	0	1
The Prior of Burton	0	2
The Lord of Alverston	0	2
The Manor of Milton	0	3
The Vavasor	0	2
John Malterson, for Wood Ansterborn (Osborne) and Chilling Wood	0	3
The Manor of Pagham	0	2
The Manor of Nettleston	0	2
The Abbot of Beaulieu	0	2
John Wyvill	0	4
John Norreys	0	1
Edward Barnaby	0	1
The Manor of Nunwell	0	2
Richard de Hale	0	2
Ralf Overton, for Horringford	0	1
Thomas Hacket	0	1
William Urry	0	1
The Lady Mary Buteler, for Hale	0	1
The Prior of Portsmouth	0	2
Geoffry Rouelle	0	2

The

	ARM.	SAG.
The Manor of Bathingborne	0	2
John Palmer of Wotton, and John Stone	0	1
Roger Baker	0	1
William Stouer	0	1
Isabell Keynis, for Niton	0	2
John Waite	0	1
Henry Pedder, for Westbrooke	0	1
Sir Theobald Gorges, for Chillingwood	0	1
The Tenant of ———	0	1
Robert Syngdone	0	1
Sir John de Kyngston, for Lucelo and Priffloe	0	1

The Churches of East Medine:

	ARM.	SAG.
The Church of Brading	2	●
Yaverland	0	1
Newchurch	2	0
Arreton	1	3
Whippingham	0	2
Niton	0	1
Benstede	0	1
Shentlyn	0	1
Bonechurch	0	1
Wootton	0	1
Wathe	0	1
Appulderford	0	1
Stownam, or Standen	0	1

The

HISTORY OF THE ISLE OF WIGHT.

	ARM.	SAG.
The Church of Knighton	0	1
———— Alverston	0	1
The Vicar of Brading	0	1
———— Arreton	0	1
———— Goddeshill	0	1
The Chapel of St. Edmund, at Wootton	0	1

The West Medine:

	ARM.	SAG.
The Prior of Carisbrooke	6	0
The Procurator of Lyra	1	2
Giles Beauchamp, for Freshwater	2	0
Gilbert de Spencer	1	2
The Lord of Affeton	1	0
The Erle of Salisbury	3	2
Sir John de Kingston	1	2
John de Compton	0	2
Sir Thomas Langford	0	3
The Manors of Gatcomb, Whitwell, Caulborn, and Mersten	3	0
Thomas Rale	1	0
Sr. Lawrence de St. Martin	1	1
The Lord of Motteston	1	0
Ralph de Woolverton	0	2
Nicholas de Woolverton	0	1
Ralf Dicton and Tho. Hacket, for Hatherfield	0	2
Sr. John Tychborn	0	2

Thomas

	ARM.	SAC.
Thomas le Wayte	0	2
William Paffelew and Geoffry Ronele	0	2
John Berle	0	2
John Fauterby	0	2
Lady Ifabella Hunfton	0	2
Henry Tailour	0	1
The Abbefs of Laycock	0	1
Park	0	2
Lawrence Ruffel	0	3

The Churches of the Weſt Medine :

	ARM.	SAC.
The Church of Freſhwater	1	9
Schaldeflet	1	9
Caulborn	1	9
Brixton	1	2
Shorewell	0	2
Gatecomb	0	3
Chale	0	2
Motteſton	0	2
Broke	0	1
Lemerſton	0	1
Kingſton	0	1
Yarmouth	0	1
The Vicar of Shorewell	0	2
Shaldeflet	0	2
Thorley	0	1

The

	ARM.	SAG.
The Vicar of Carefbrook	0	2
The Prior of Chriftchurch, who is Rector of Thorley*	0	1

In all, fifty-four men at arms, and one hundred and forty-two bowmen. Thefe, however, by no means conftituted the whole force of the ifland at this period, fince a kind of *general militia* was furnifhed by the feveral parifhes and tythings, in cafes of external affault, which was diftributed into companies, and commanded by fuch lords of manors as were of the moft approved military fkill: and if thefe refources were infufficient for its protection, the warden had ftill a difcretionary power vefted in him, of levying new forces throughout the ifland, and of impreffing men for its defence from the County of Southampton.†

To thefe regulations for its fafety, the Ifle of Wight continued fubject for the fpace of many

---

* Sir R. Worfley's Hift. Ifle of Wight, Append. No. II.

† Rot. Franc. 26. Ed. III. m. 13.

years, till Henry VIII. incenfed by fome recent defcents of the French on the Britifh coaft, adopted the plan of building a number of forts and block-houfes on the parts moft expofed to their infults. Thofe erected at this time, on the ifland, were the following :*

Sandown Fort, fituated at the bottom of a bay of that name, in the South-eaftern part of the ifland.†

Yarmouth Caftle, intended to defend the entrance of the river *Yar*,‡ on the north-weftern part.

Worfley's Tower, (long fince demolifhed) built on a point of land, about a mile to the Weft of Yarmouth.

* Thefe were all built about the 36th Hen. VIII.

† This fortrefs is ftill kept in repair, and has the following eftablifhment :—A captain, twelve warders, one mafter gunner, three other gunners. It is a regular quadrilateral building; having a baftion at each angle, and furrounded with a wet ditch.

‡ Yar, is a corruption of yr, a Britifh appellative for water. The eftablifhment of this caftle is ftill preferved; though its ufes have long fince ceafed. It has a captain, one mafter gunner, and five other gunners.

Weft

West Cowes Castle, erected on the West side of the river Medina, on the North shore of the island, and *East Cowes Castle*, on the other side of the same river, of which no vestige now remains.*

The establishment of Sandham and West-Cowes castles, will appear from the underwritten account of fees paid to their respective garrisons:

Sandham Castle, Sandham Bay.

PER DIEM.

4s. Captain
2s. Under ditto
6d. Soldiers, thirteen
8d. Porters, one
8d. Master Gunner
6d. Other Gunners, seven

} Fee £363 6s. 8d.

West - Cowes Fortress.

1s. Captain
6d. Soldiers, two
8d. Porter, one
6d. Gunners, six

} Fee £103 8s. 4d.†

---

* West Cowes castle is also utterly useless; but still has a captain, one master gunner, and five other gunners.

† Sir R. Worsley's Hist. Append. No. XXXVI.

The nature and proportions of the military stores kept in the different castles of the island, at the period of Henry's death, are still preserved to us, and may be deemed sufficiently curious to be laid before the reader.

The Isle of Wight.*

The Castell at Yarmouthe. } Ordenaunce, artillery, and other munycions of warre remaynyng at the saide castell in the custody and chardge of Richard Edwall, captaine there, the 26th. of Decembre, anno regni regis nunc Edwardi sexti primo.

Curtall Cannon of Brasse furnyshed	Oone
Demy Culveryne of Brasse furnyshed	Oone
Demy Culveryne of caste Irone furnyshed	Oone
Fowlers of Irone with 4 chambers stocks broken	ij°.
Sacres of Caste Irone furnyshed	ij°.

* Extracted from a MS. formerly in the possession of Gustavus Brander, Esq. (now in the British Museum), being " An inventory of the plate, jewells, ordenaunce, &c. of Henry VIII." dated 14th September, 1547.

Doble

Doble barces of yrone with iiij chambers	ij°.
Single bafes of yrone with iiij chambers	ij°.
Demy culveryne of cafte yrone	- Oone broken.
Cannon fhot of yrone	xv.
Demy culveryne Shott of yrone	xlvj.
Sacre fhotte of yrone	c.
Fowler fhotte of ftone	l^{ti}.
Shotte of doble bafes of diece and lead	l^{ti}.
Shott of fingle bafes	xxx^{ti}.
Serpentyne powder	viij di. bar. iij doble.
Hagbuttes furnyfhed	xix.
Corne Powder for the fame	di°. Bar.
Bowes	cxl^{ti}-
Sheiffs of Arrows	ccxlviij.
Bowftrings oone firkyne, conteyning	ij Groffe.
Billes	ccxxiij.

The Block-houfe at Sharpnode within the faid Ifle of Wight, in the charge of Nicholas Cheke.

Demy Culveryns of Braffe furnyfhed	Oone
Sacres of Braffe furnyfhed	Oone
Demy culveryne fhotte of yrone	xxj.

Sacre

Sacre Shotte of yrone - - xxiij.
Serpentyne powder - - Oone doble Bar.

The Caſtell of } Ordenaunce, artyllery, and
Caryſbrooke. } other munycions of warre remayninge at the ſaid Caſtell in the cuſtody and charge of Richard Worſley gentilman, Captayne of the ſaid iſle.

Slynges of yrone furnyſhed - - ij°.
Fowler of yrone furnyſhed - - Oone.
Doble baſſys of yron furnyſhed - ij°.
Hoole culveryne ſhotte - - xxx^{ti}.
Demy Cannon Shotte - - l^{ti}.
Yron for divers peices - - xxxtⁱ.
Demy culveryne Shotte of yrone - xxx^{ti}.
Sacre ſhotte of Yrone - - cciiij.
Fawcon ſhotte of yrone - - clx^{ti}.
Doble baſis ſhotte - - xl^{ti}.
Serpentyne powder - - { xxiij doble bar. iij. firk.
Hagbuttes furnyſhed, lacking xx flaſks and xx touch-boxes } cxl.
Coilles of Lyntte - - - DC.
Corne Powder - - - iiij doble bar.
Cheſtes

Chestes of Arrowes	lix.
Chestes of Bowes	xxi.
Bow strings	iij Bar.
Morispickes	D.
Javelyns	c. iiij. iiij. (xx over iiij)
Billes	Dccl.

The Castell of Sandham baye.

Ordenaunce, artillery, and other munycions of warre remaynyng at the said castell in the custody and charge of Peter Smythe Captayne there.

Demy culveryns of brasse furnyshed	Oone.
Saker of brasse furnyshed	Oone.
Fawcone of brasse furnyshed	Oone.
Porte pieces of yrone with ii chambers furnyshed	Oone.
Hoole slynges of yrone furnyshed	Oone.
Demy slynges of yrone with vi chambers	v.
Quarter Slynges of yrone with oone chamber	Oone.
Demy Culveryn shotte of yrone	iiij. (xx over)
Demy culveryn shotte of dice and lead	xv.

Hollow

Hollow shottes for wild fier - -	xij.
Sacre shotte of yrone - -	lxij.
Sacre shotte of Dice and Leade -	iiij.xx xiiij.
Fawcon shotte of yrone - -	xxxvj.
Fawcon shotte of Dice and leade -	cxvj.
Shotte of stone for port pieces -	xxiiij.
Cases of haile shotte for the same -	xxvijj.
Slynge shotte of Dice and leade - -	xij.
Demy flyng shotte of Dice and Leade	c.
Quarter flynge shotte of dice and leade	xlvj.
Serpentyne powder -	{ iij doble bar. j firk.
Hagbushes wanting flasks and touch-boxes	lxxviij.
Corne powder - - -	Oone firk.
Bowes - - - -	Oone chest.
Sheiff Arrowes - - -	Oone chest.
Pickes - - - -	cl.
Billes - - - -	cxx.

The Castell at the Weste Cowe.

Ordenaunce, artillery, and other munycions of Warre remaynyng in the said castell in the charge or custody of Robert Raymonde Captayne.

The

HISTORY OF THE ISLE OF WIGHT. 73

The Barbycan.

Curtoll cannon of Braffe furnyfhed -	Oone
Baftard Culveryne of Braffe furnyfhed	Oone
Porte pieces of yrone furnyfhed with iiij chambers	ij.
Three Quarter Slynges with ij chambers	Oone.
Porte pieces not able to ferve -	Oone.
Cannon Shotte of yrone - -	xvij.
Baftard Culveryn Shotte of yrone -	xiij.
Baftard Culveryn Shotte of leade -	lvj.
Shotte for port pieces of Stone -	xxx.
Slinge Shotte of Irone - -	xxxij.

The Wefte Wynge.

Doble bafes with ij chambers not hable to ferve	Oone.
Single bafes with iij chambers not hable to ferve	ij.

The Eafte Winge.

Doble bafes with iij chambers not hable to ferve	ij.

L The

The mayne Towre.

Doble bafes with ii chambers furnyfhed	Oone.
Three quarter Slinges with ii chambers apiece, whereof oone is not hable to ferve	iij.
Single Bafes with viij chambers not hable to ferve	iiij.
Three quarter fling fhott of leade	cxlvj.
Shotte for doble bafes	lxiiij.
Serpentyne Powder	j doble Bar. ij firk.
Hagbutts not hable to ferve	x.
Corne Powder	iiij lb.
Bowes	xix.
Chefts of Arrowes	xxxij.
Pickes	xxij.
Billes	xx.

In the year 1558, a very confiderable addition was made to the means of defence in the Ifle of Wight, by the introduction of *fire arms* there. Richard Worfley, Efq. who was that year reinftated in his office of captain of the ifland, received orders to put the common

mon musket of the times into the hands of the militia, and to settle an armourer at Carisbrooke castle, for the purpose of fabricating them. These directions were executed, and the soldiers received their new arms; which although they were the rude and clumsy harquebusses of the sixteenth century, with the match lock, and rest, yet they might be considered as much more formidable instruments of destruction than the weapons before in use amongst them.*

It was in consequence of these new regulations, and the vigilant care with which they were inforced, that the militia of the Isle of Wight wore a very respectable appearance towards the close of the sixteenth century. Camden speaks of the inhabitants at that time, as

---

* About the same time, the islanders voluntarily put themselves to the trouble and expence of providing a train of artillery for their defence. Each parish found one, which was either kept in a small house built for the purpose, or in some part of the church. About eighteen of these remain. The carriages and ammunition were provided at the expence of the parishes, and particular farms were charged with the duty of finding horses to draw them. Sir R. Worsley, p. 41.

excelling

excelling greatly in military skill. " They are brave and courageous," says he, " and so constantly trained by the captain of the island, as to understand completely all the operations of war. They excel in firing at a mark; can keep their ranks; march compact and orderly; or extend their files if need be; are inured to hardship, fatigue, heat and dust, and can perform every office of a soldier. The island," he continues, " can raise four thousand soldiers of its own; and can have, at a short notice, three thousand well disciplined men from Hampshire, and two thousand from Wiltshire."*

In the year 1625, the island could bring into the field, two thousand and twenty effective men; the following statement shews in what manner they were armed, and how divided into companies.

A true Noate of the Strenght of the island, taken by Sir John Oglander, liftennant, the 12th of May 1625, and by him delivered to the Counsell.

* Cam. Brit. Edit. 1607.

In

In Sir John Oglander's Band.

Officers	7
Mufketieres	60
Corflettes	21
Bare Pickes	9
Soom	97

In Sir Edward Dennis Bande.

Officers	10
Mufkettes	103
Corflettes	13
Bare Pickes	23
Men unarmed	61
Som	210

Appeldorcoombe Bande.

Officers	9
Mufkettes	150
Corflettes	25
Bare Pickes	37
Men unarmed	40
Som	261

Mr. Dillington's Band.

Officers	12
Mufkettes	60
Corflettes	

Corflettes	20
Bare Pickes	15
Men unarmed	15
Som	122

Sir John Richardes Bande.

Officers	6
Muskettes	61
Corflettes	14
Bare Pickes and men unarmed	28
Som	109

Mr. Cheekes Band.

Officers	7
Muskettes	113
Corflettes	21
Bare Pickes	13
Som	154

Sir William Meux.

Officers	12
Muskettes	156
Collivors	29
Corflettes	44
Men unarmed	20
Som	261

Mr. Leyghe's Band.

Officers	6
Muskettes	63
Corslettes	16
Bare Pickes	10
Som	95

Mr. Borman's Band.

Officers	13
Muskettes	65
Corslettes	17
Bare Pickes	20
Som	115

Mr. Hobson's Band.

Officers	18
Muskettes	83
Corslettes	38
Men unarmed	31
Som	170

Mr. Urrie's Band.

Officers	11
Muskettes	80
Corslettes	

Corflettes	22
Bare Pickes	9
Soom	122

Nuport Band.

Officers	22
Muskettes	94
Collivors	4
Corflettes	12
Bare pickes	32
Holberdes	10
Men unarmed	130
Som	304

Muskettes	1088
Collivors	33
Corflettes	263
Bare Pickes	196
Holberdes	10
Men unarmed	297
Officers	133
Som totoll of all the able men within the Island is.	2020

Since they arr all armed.*

* Sir Richard Worsley's Hist. Append. No. XIV.

Three

Three years after the return of this statement, the above force was new-modelled, and formed into sixteen companies, which were, in the year 1638, commanded and appointed to the stations as under.

The Watches and Wardes that ar now kept in our Island. Sep. 20. 1638.

East Meden.

Captain Rice { At St. Caterons, a Ward with 2 Men.
On the Hatton Nyghtonfyld, a watch with 2 men.

Sir Ed. Dennys { A Watch at Lanes, 2 Men.
A Ward at Roxall Down.

Sir J. Oglander { Ashen Down, a Ward one Man and a Watch 2 Men.
At St. Helen's poynt, a watch, 2 men.

Sir R. Dillington { On Knyghton, a Watch, 2 Men.
At Ryde, a Watch, 2 men.

Sir Hen. Worseley { At Apeldercombe, a watch 2 men
At Criple at Nyghton, a watch, 2 men.

M   Cap.

Cap. Cheeke	At St. George's Down, a Watch 2 men.
Cap. Bafkett	On Binbridge Down, a ward, one Man, and a Watch, 2 men.
Sir Wm. Liflie	At Eaſt Cowes, Wootton poynt, and at Fifchowfe, a Watch, 2 men a peece.

Weſt Meden.

Mr. Mewx	At Ramfe Down, a watch 2 men. At Chale Down, a watch, 2 men.
Sir John Leygh	At Lardon Down, a watch, 2 men. At Atherfylde, a watch, 2 men.
Cap. Urry	On Hearberoe Down, a Ward, 2 Men On the feae ſhore at Brixton, a watch, 2 men.
Cap. Harvye	On Avington Downe, a Watch, 2 Men. At Northwood, a Watch, 2 Men, On Gatecombe Downe, a watch, 2 Men.
Cap. Booreman	On Frefchewaltor Downe, a ward and Watch, two men apeece. On Motfon Downe, a Watch, 2 Men.

Cap.

Cap. Hobſon   At Hamſtede, a Watch, 2 Men.
Newport 2 Com- }
panies.   } They only watch in the towne.

The internal ſtrength of the iſland, however, ſeems to have fallen off conſiderably in the courſe of a very few years after this arrangement of its militia; for on the appointment of the Earl of Pembroke to the government of it, in 1642, a repreſentation of its ſtate was tranſmitted by Sir John Dingley (who had been deputy-governor) to that nobleman, which affirms that the train-bands were very much weakened and decayed, and if there were not a ſpeedy courſe taken, would be daily worſe and worſe; on account of the lords of the manors taking their copyholds into their own hands as quickly as they fell in; and the rich farmers laying together all the farms they could put their hands upon; cauſes which occaſioned a ſenſible decreaſe in the population and ſtrength of the iſland.

Further regulations were adopted ſoon after the above repreſentation, and in the year 1651

M 2   a ſet

a set of instructions was delivered to the militia of the island, of a very sensible nature; comprizing a long list of precautions to be taken, for the prevention of an enemy's landing, or for resisting him if he did land. A copy of these instructions was sent to every captain, with orders to have them read at the head of his company whenever it was mustered.*

Immediately on the restoration of Charles the Second, Lord Culpeper was appointed governor of the island; whose inattention with respect to the means of its defence, and arbitrary proceedings in civil matters, induced the inhabitants to present a petition to the king for his removal; in which they state, that the ancient magazines and stores of the island, were neither so full, nor in so good repair as in former times; nor the militia in such a condition as was consistent with the safety of the place.

In the lord chancellor's answer to this petition, it is promised, that Lord Culpeper should

* Sir R. Worsley's Append. No. XVIII.

be

be forthwith difpatched to the ifland to regulate its militia, and order matters for its better fecurity. This, however, he had not an opportunity of doing, as he fhortly after refigned his poft of governor; in which he was fucceeded by Sir Robert Holmes.

In the year 1757 the prefent militia of the Ifle of Wight was firft raifed; and drawn out, embodied, and formed into an independent company in 1770. It confifts of fixty men, and is commanded by a captain under the governor.

This ifland has alfo lately evinced its patriotifm, in the formation of a cavalry corps, confifting of fifty men (officers included) denominated *The Loyal Ifle of Wight Yeomanry Cavalry;* a corps raifed for the repulfion of foreign attack, and the fuppreffion of domeftic confufion.

THE

ECCLESIASTICAL HISTORY

OF THE

ISLE OF WIGHT.

CHAP. I.

OF THE ANCIENT RELIGION OF THE ISLE OF WIGHT, AND THE INTRODUCTION OF CHRISTIANITY THERE.

DRUIDISM was the ancient religion of the Isle of Wight. Both its original Celtic inhabitants, and their Belgic succeffors, profeffed this mode of worfhip.

The Druid doctrine, in its primeval state, was sublime and simple. It taught the exiftence of one eternal, almighty God, the Creator and Ruler of the univerfe, to whom all things were subject and obedient.* It taught also

* Regnator omnium. DEUS, cætera subjecta atque parentia.—Tacit.

the

the immortality of the soul; that great principle, which is the most effectual spur to virtue, the greatest check to vice, and happiest antidote to despair.† It further inculcated, the belief of a future state, in which the spirits of the departed were to be cloathed with incorruptible bodies, unfading youth, and perpetual beauty; and invited its followers to rectitude in peace, and gallantry in war, by prospects of an unceasing repetition of those pleasures (though infinitely exalted and refined), in the island of the West,* which they had most esteemed and delighted in, during their residence on earth.‡

† Ενισχύει γαρ παρ' αυτοῖς ὁ Πυθαγόρου λογος, ὅτι τας ψυχὰς τῶν ἀνθρώπων ἀθανάτους εἶναι συμβέβηκε. Diod. Sic. lib. V.
Imprimis hoc volunt persuadere, non interire animas. —Cæs. lib. VI. c. xiv.

* Celebratæ illæ beatorum insulæ dicuntur esse in Occidentali oceano.—Eustathius ad Dion. Perieg.

‡ Vobis auctoribus, umbræ,
Non tacitas Erebi sedes, Ditisque profundi
Pallida Regna petunt; regit idem spiritus artus
Orbe alio: longæ (canitis si cognita) vitæ
Mors media est.
      Lucani Pharf. lib. I.

Thus

Thus simple and noble was the Druidical religion originally; before the ignorance, the errors, and the fears of the multitude, had corrupted and diftorted its philofophical tenets. The policy of its minifters, the Druids, however, involved thefe truths in wilful obfcurity, and in order to preferve their empire over the public mind, they wrapped themfelves and their doctrine in the mantle of myftery. This conduct naturally increafed their own importance and the veneration of their followers; but at the fame time, left the latter to the wild wanderings of gloomy fuperftition; to the frightful confequences of affociated folly, ignorance, and vice. The effects were fuch as might be expected; the people degenerated into the groffeft Polytheifm;* immoralities of the impureft nature were univerfally practifed

* Deorum maximè Mercurium colunt, cui certis diebus humanis quoque hoftiis litare fas habent.—Tacit. de Mor. Germ. c. ix..

 Et quibus immitis placatur fanguine diro
 Tentates, horrenfque feris altaribus *Hefus*,
 Et *Taranis* Scythicæ non mitior ara Dianæ.
        Lucan, lib. i.

amongft

amongſt them;* and they heſitated not at appeaſing their multifarious deities by human ſacrifices.†

Such was the ſtate of religion in the Iſle of Wight when the Romans arrived there; a ſyſtem which it would be one of their firſt objects to overturn, for they wiſely concluded that whilſt its prieſts retained that dominion over the minds of the people, which the terrors of their doctrine had acquired to them, patient ſubmiſſion, quiet government, and public order could never be expected. They therefore (with reſpect to Britain) departed from their eſtabliſhed maxim, *of adopting the deities of the conquered nations*, and never ceaſed from religious perſecution, till not a veſtige of Druidiſm remained.‡

---

* Uxores habent deni duodenique inter ſe communes, et maximè fratres cum fratribus, et parentes cum liberis.—Cæſar, p. 89.

† Cæſar, p. 120.

‡ Tacit. Ann. lib. XIV. c. xxx.

The

The splendid and motley, but more humane religion of Rome, was now introduced into the Isle of Wight; and we may suppose some temples would necessarily be reared there, by a people, who animated every virtue and vice, every passion and attribute of the mind, and even every abstracted idea, into a living divinity.

But the happy period now approached, when the refulgence of the Gospel was to disperse the moral darkness of the British empire; to illuminate the understandings, and purify the hearts of those, who had hitherto been wrapped in the gloom of Pagan superstition. Towards the conclusion of the first century after our Saviour's birth, the religion of Christ was received in England, and in the course of a few years, traversed a great part of the Southern coast; so that we may fairly conclude, by the beginning of the second century, the blessings, advantages, and comforts of Christianity were offered to, and accepted by the inhabitants of the Isle of Wight.

When, however, this district yielded to the fury of a new invader, and became the acquisition

quisition of the Saxons, it changed its religion with its inhabitants, and once more witnessed the follies of Paganism.

The religion of the Saxons was that of a barbarous, fierce, and sensual people; gross and gloomy. Their deities were clothed with terrors and vengeance, and only to be appeased by the blood of human offerings. The fancied pleasures of Odin's Hall too, the seat of the departed warrior, were such as suited the depraved conceptions of an illiterate, unenlightened people, whose sole delights were feasting, slaughter, and the chace. In this mansion of happiness, the chief, who perished in battle, quaffed his favorite ale from the skulls of his enemies.[*] He appeased his hunger with the fat of the inexhaustible wild boar *Serimner*, which was renewed, as soon as carved from the immortal animal.[†] Again he experienced the extacy of

[*] In craniis inimicorum brevi bibam in præstantis Odini aulâ.—Epiced. Reg. Lodbrog apud Bartholin.

[†] Mallet's Northern Antiquities, vol. II. Edda, Fable 20th.

the chace in the purfuit of airy ftags;‡ and had the daily felicity of mingling in battle, and falling, together with his opponent, tranffixed by mutual wounds.§ A death, however, which was only to be temporary; for when dinner was announced, the fpiritual forms of the flaughtered warriors were once more animated; they again mounted their fteeds, and rode unhurt into Valhalla, where frefh recruits of fat and ale invited them to the diurnal debauch.*

Thus vicious, wild, and abfurd, were the religious fancies of our Saxon anceftors; before the rays of Chriftianity had enlightened their darkling reafon, and purified their grofs conceptions.

It muft be confeffed, however, that depraved as thefe notions were, they were probably the

‡ Offian. v. I. p. 54.

§ Mallet's North. Antiq. ut fupra.

* Inftanti verò prandii tempori omnes incolumes in aulam equitant, et ad potandum confident. Edda, Mythog. xxxv. Apud Mallet, ut fupra.

foundation

foundation of that enthufiaftic valor and contempt of death, which ftrongly marked their character, and rendered their conqueft of Britain complete. Men who could firmly perfuade themfelves, that deftruction in the field of battle would be followed by an endlefs fruition of delight, would rather court, than fhun the enemy's fword. Their religious prejudices would teach them to defpife danger in all its fhapes, and convert death, which moft other fyftems of religion involve with terrors, into a defirable event—a paffport to immortality and joy.*

Towards the latter end of the feventh century, the Ifle of Wight was once more liberated from Pagan fuperftition; though the circumftances of its converfion to Chriftianity were fomewhat harfh and cruel. Bede thus relates the particulars: "As foon as Ceadwalla had poffeffed

---

* Certè populi quos defpicit Arctos
Felices errore fuo! quos ille timorum
Maximus haud urget lethi metus; *inde* ruendi
In ferrum mens prona viris, animæque capaces
Mortis; et ignavum rediturx parcere vitæ.
      Lucan, Pharf. lib. I.

himfelf

himself of the kingdom of the Gevissii, he took also the Isle of Wight, which hitherto (i. e. since it had been in the possession of the Saxons) had been devoted to idolatry. He formed a resolution to massacre all its inhabitants, and place in their room people of his own province, binding himself by a vow, (though he himself was not yet converted to Christianity,) if he gained the island, to devote a fourth part of it, and its spoils to the Lord. This he performed, by granting it to Bishop Wilfred, who happened to be here at the time from his own country. The extent of this island, according to the estimation of the English, is equal to the support of one thousand two hundred families. The Bishop had the land of three hundred given him. This portion he committed to one of his clergy, named *Bernwin*, his sister's son, allowing him a priest, named *Hildila*, to instruct and baptize all that offered themselves. I must not here omit, that among the first fruits of those who were saved by their faith here, two infant brothers of *Aruandus*, king of the island, obtained the crown of martyrdom, by the special

grace

grace of God. On the enemy's approach they escaped out of the island, and were conveyed to the adjoining country, where being conducted to the place called *Ad Lapidem*,* and thinking there to conceal themselves from the victorious monarch, they were betrayed, and ordered to be put to death. A certain abbot and priest named *Cynbreth*, who had a monastery not far off, at a place called Reodford,† or the Ford of Reeds, hearing of it, came to the king (who was concealed in the same neighbourhood, to have his wounds dressed, which he had received in battle in the Isle of Wight,) and besought him that if the lads must die, they might first receive Baptism. The king granted his request; and he instructing them in the word of truth, and washing them in the fountain of life, secured their admission into the king-

---

* Probably, *Stone*, a manor in the parish of Fawley; near the sea shore, and immediately opposite the Isle of Wight.

† The ancient name of Red-bridge; where, in the Saxon times was a religious house. — Tanner's Not. Monastica.

dom

dom of Heaven. When the executioner came, they gladly submitted to temporal death, by which they doubted not to pass to eternal life. In this manner," continues Bede, " after all the provinces of Britain had embraced Christianity, the Isle of Wight received it also."*

* Bede, lib. VI. 16. Gough's Camden, vol. I. p. 124.

CHAP. II.

OF THE RELIGIOUS FOUNDATIONS IN THE ISLE OF WIGHT.

It is seldom found that any religion receives improvement from time; but on the contrary, that as it gains age it acquires corruption. Being an universal concern, it is in the hands of all; and the follies and superstitions of some, the vices and prejudices of others, will, in the natural course of things, soon vitiate and deform it. Such was the case with the purest, simplest, and best of all religions; and *Christianity* in a very few ages after the apostolical times, had, by the ignorance or perverseness of its professors, been stripped of almost all those divine graces, which adorned it when first promulgated to mankind. Errors innumerable, both in doctrine and practice, darkened the whole Christian world. Monstrous and impious absurdities disgraced its worship. The spirit of religion entirely evaporated, and riseless ridiculous ceremonies were substituted in the room of real piety.* In this state of religious depravity,

* The following is the picture of a *good christian*, in the seventh century, as drawn by a *saint* of that age; by which we discover that, in the opinions of those times, a man might be deemed extremely pious, and reckon himself sure of heaven, without the trouble of fulfilling one single duty towards God or his neighbour. "Bonus Christianus est qui ad ecclesiam frequenter venit, et oblationem, quæ in altari Deo offeratur, exhibet; qui de fructibus suis non gustat, nisi prius Deo aliquid offerat; qui, quoties sanctæ solemnitates adveniunt, ante dies plures castitatem etiam cum propriâ uxore, ut securâ conscientiâ Domini altare accedere possit; qui, postremò, symbolum vel orationem Dominicam numeriter tenet. Redimite animas vestras de pœnâ, dum habetis in potestate remedia: oblationes et decimas ecclesiæ offerte; luminaria sanctis locis, juxta quod habetis, exhibete; ad ecclesiam quoque frequentiùs convenite; sanctorum patrocinia humiliter expetite: quod si observaveritis, securi in die judicii ante tribunal æterni judicis venientes, dicetis, ' Da, Domine, quia dedimus,' &c."—Vita Sancti Eligii in Dacherii Spicileg. Vet. Scrip. vol. II.

the obligations of morality would of courſe be but little attended to; and in faƈt we find, that, during the *middle ages*, as they are called, (from the ninth to the twelfth century, when this mantle of mental darkneſs was moſt cloſely drawn over Chriſtendom) the different offices, relations, and duties of life were leſs underſtood, and worſe fulfilled, than at any other period of time. During this gloomy interval, many ſtrange opinions aroſe, and amongſt the reſt, that the prayers of *others* might be as efficacicus in averting the wrath of Heaven from a ſinner, as his own devotions; or, in other words, that it was poſſible to be *pious by proxy*. A principle like this, which reconciled temporal licentiouſneſs with eternal felicity, and permitted a free ſcope to the paſſions without annexing the terrors of future puniſhment to their indulgence, met with a welcome reception; and ſinners of affluence and rank immediately began founding religious houſes for the reception of thoſe who were thus to be their *proxies* in the works of prayer and godlineſs. Hence aroſe the numerous monaſteries which

were

were thickly sprinkled in every country throughout the Christian world, before the close of the seventh century; and for several ages afterwards increased with a rapidity only to be accounted for by the *natural* of the *opinions* which gave them birth originally.

The Normans, a fierce and profligate people, were deeply tinctured with these superstitions and delusive notions; and as soon as they had acquired England, began with all expedition, founding abbies and monasteries throughout the kingdom. William Fitz-Osborne, on whom the Isle of Wight was bestowed, followed the example of his countrymen, and founded the priory of Carisbrook. The history of this religious house is very concise.

Baldwin de Redvers, Earl of Devon, in the reign of King Stephen, grants the church of Carisbrook (after the death of two persons mentioned in his deed) to the abbot and convent of Lyra (in Normandy), to be freely by them enjoyed, either as demesne, or they might send monks to the said church.

A grant

A grant and confirmation of William de Vernun, in the reign of king John, occurs, by which the church of Carifbrook is to receive two marks per annum, out of the toll of the ifland; on the condition of the monks performing daily fervice in the chapel of Newport.

A general charter of confirmation ratifies to the abbot and convent of Lyra in Normandy, the church of Carifbrook, with divers other chapels and churches in the ifland.

Edward III. when he made his ill-founded claims to the crown of France, feized upon Carifbrook, and all its churches, as an alien priory; and granted it to the abbey of Mont Grace, in Yorkfhire. Henry IV. however, immediately on coming to the crown, reftored it with many others to the former poffeffors.

Henry V. again refumed it, and granted it to the monaftery of Shene in Surry, where it continued till the diffolution. In the reign of Henry VIII. this monaftery was leafed to Sir James Worfley; from the widow of whofe

fon,

son, it came to Sir Francis Walsingham. Sir Thomas Fleming afterwards made a purchase of it; and through his descendents it devolved to the present possessors; the vicarage remaining in the crown till the time of Charles I. who gave it to Queen's College, Oxford. The chapels of Northwood, West Cowes, and Newport, belong to the church of Carisbrook.*

The abbey of Quarr, or De Quarreira† as it was anciently called, owes its origin to Baldwin Earl of Devon, who in the thirty-second year of Henry I. gave the manor of Arreton to Geoffry, abbot of Savigny in Normandy, for the building of this monastery, which was dedicated to St. Mary. This abbey appears to have been richly endowed, and that too, by personages of the first consequence; several of whom made it the place of their interment. Amongst these were its founder, Earl Baldwin, Adeliza his countess, and Henry

* Sir Rich. Worsley's Hist. p. 163, et infra.

† Probably from its neighbouring stone quarries. It was of the Cistertian order.

their

their son; William de Vernun, who bequeathed three hundred pounds (a prodigious sum in the thirteenth century) for the erection of a monument to himself, his lady; and the lady Cicely, second daughter of Edward IV.

In the fifteenth century the lands of Quarr Abbey, were taxed as follows:

" De Redditu assis. taxat. ad - viij marks.
" Apud Newnham ad - - xv m.
" Apud Sambele (Combley) ad - xvj m.
" Apud Arreton, ad - - xviij m.
" Virga de Bykeburie (Bugbury) ad lx s.
" Apud Haffeley, ad - - xviij m.
" Apud Lovecomb, ad - - xij m.
" Apud Staplehurst et Claybrooke - xl s.
" Apud Roweburg - - l s.
" Apud Schete - - - vij m.
" Apud Shalcomb & Compton - x m.
" Apud Beneftede - - xl s.
" Apud Foxore - - - lviij s.
" Apud Schrob & Goy, ad - xlij s.
" De duobus molendinis apud x^{ti} ecclesiam xij s.
" De 4 Molendinis in Ins. Vecta - xv s.

" De

" De Proventu tannaria - - xl s.
" Sm. ii̅i̅j̅. xvj*l*. iij*s*. iiij*d*. Inde decima ix*l*. xij*s*. iiij*d*."*

After the diffolution of Quarr. Abbey it was purchafed by a Mr. George Mills of Southampton, who, for the fake of its materials, fo completely dilapidated it, that very few of the remains have reached our time.

The fituation of this religious houfe is a very pleafing and fecluded one; commanding a charming view of the water, and deeply embofomed in woods.

Towards the clofe of the thirteenth century, the oratory of Burton was founded by John de Infula, Rector of Shalfleet, and Thomas de Winton, Rector of Godfhill; and regulated by the following ftatutes:

1. That there fhall be fix chaplains and one clerk to officiate both for the living and the dead under the rules of St. Auguftine.

2. That one of thefe fhall be prefented to the Bifhop of Winchefter, to be the arch-

* Sir R. Worfley, 176.

prieft; to whom the reft-fhall take an oath of obedience.

3. That the arch-prieft fhall be chofen by the chaplains there refiding, who fhall prefent him to the bifhop within twenty days after any vacancy fhall happen.

4. That they fhall be fubject to the immediate authority of the bifhop.

5. When any chaplain fhall die, his goods fhall remain to the oratory.

6. They fhall have only one mefs, with a pittance, at a meal, excepting on the greater feftivals, when they may have three meffes.

7. They fhall be diligent in reading and praying.

8. They fhall not go beyond the bounds of the oratory, without licence from the arch-prieft.

9. Their habit fhall be of one colour, either black or blue; they fhall be cloathed *pallio Hibernienfi, de nigra boneta cum pileo.*

10. The arch-prieft fhall fit at the head of the table; next to him thofe who have celebrated

brated magnam miffam; then the prieft of St. Mary; next the prieft of the Holy Trinity; and then the prieft who fays mafs for the dead.

11. The clerk fhall read fomething edifying to them while they dine.

12. They fhall fleep in one room.

13. They fhall ufe a fpecial prayer for their benefactors.

14. They fhall in all their ceremonies, and in tinkling the bell, follow the ufe of Sarum.

15. The arch-prieft alone fhall have charge of the bufinefs of the houfe.

16. They fhall, all of them, at their admiffion into the houfe, fwear to the obfervance of thefe ftatutes.

As foon as the fociety was eftablifhed, the founders granted the patronage of the oratory to John, Bifhop of Winchefter, and his fucceffors, that he might become a protector and defender of them, the arch-prieft, and his fellow-chaplains.

In the Eighteenth of Henry VI. this religious houfe was entirely furrendered into the hands of the Bishop of Winchester; and, together with its lands, granted to Winchester College; under which society, the site and demesnes of the oratory are still held.*

There appears to have been a small priory at St. Helen's, belonging to some abbey in France, of the Cluniac order. It is supposed to have been founded soon after the conquest; but by whom is not known. It was one of the alien priories given by Henry VI. to his college at Eton, of whose possessions it is still a part.†

The Priory of Appuldurcombe was founded and made a cell to the Abbey of Montsburg in Normandy, by Richard de Redvers, founder

* Worsley, 177 et infra.

† There was a small church at St. Helen's built by the convent, who supplied it from their own community, till such time as the canons required resident vicars. In Cardinal Beaufort's valuation the church is rated at thirty marks. The old church was situated so near the sea, that the waves carried off part of the building. A brief was obtained in 1719 and a new church erected in a more convenient spot.—St. Helen's is a vicarage; patron, Eton College. Church dedicated to St. Helena.

of that abbey. The latter monaftery placed a prior, and two monks here, to receive the profits of their lands. King Henry IV. during a war with France, prefented the priory and its demefnes, which were Appuldurcombe, Sandford, and Week, to the nuns without Aldgate, London; who afterwards obtained a confirmation of the lands from the abbey of Montfburgh. The Bifhop of Winchefter being ordered, tempore Edward III, and during the war with France, to remove the religious belonging to the alien monafteries, to Hyde Abbey near Winchefter; the prior and two monks were fent thither from Appuldurcombe.*

The priory of St. Crofs, near Newport, was a cell to the abbey of Tyrone in France, and probably an hofpital. Its founder is unknown. Being an alien priory, it was feized by the crown, and given to the college of Winchefter, which ftill poffeffes it.

In the parifh of Northwood, alfo, was a religious houfe, confifting of " Brothers and

* Worfley, 181.

Sifters

Sisters of the Fraternity of St. John the Baptist;" and under the control and regulation of certain officers called *Seneschalles,* or stewards. It was founded at the latter end of Henry the Seventh's reign, and suppressed by his successor.

There were also several other *small* charitable and religious foundations in the Isle of Wight, of many of which scarcely more than the names remain. They were as follow:

1. A chapel dedicated to St. Austin, belonging to Carisbrook priory, for lepers.

2. A chapel for the infirm, licensed by the bishop, who gave the appointment of the chaplain to the abbot of Lyra.

3. A chapel was built at Knighton, in the year 1301, by Sir Ralph de Gorges, Lord of that manor; and was often presented to by his family.

4. The Lisle family, Lords of Appleford, erected a chapel on that manor. Sir John Lisle presented to it in the year 1331, and Sir Bartholemew Lisle in the year 1344.

5. Walter

5. Walter de Godyton founded St. Catherine's, a chapel on Chale Down, in the year 1323.

6. The chantry at Gatcombe was a chapel in the church at Whitwell, dedicated to St. Radigund; founder unknown.

7. Brennew was a small chapel in the parish of Freshwater. In a valuation of the spiritualities in the Diocese of Winchester, made in the time of Cardinal Beaufort, this chapel is taxed at one mark.

8. Woolverton,
9. Middleton,
10. La Wode,

These three chapels belonged to the lordship of Bimbridge, wherein they were situated; which, with the advowson of the chapels, were granted away in the forty-fixth year of Edward III. They do not appear to have been endowed.

11. A chantry at Newport, dedicated to the Virgin Mary, and founded by John Garston of that town.

12. A chapel de Sancto Licio, mentioned in Cardinal Beaufort's valuation, but exempted as insignificant.

We

We shall conclude this summary of the Ecclesiastical History of the Isle of Wight, with a concise account of its existing churches.*

Brading church, the oldest in the island, was built in the Saxon times. Its advowson being contested at law, in the thirty-seventh year of Henry III. between the abbot of Wenlock, and Walter Lisle and Maud his wife, the point was tried, and a decision passed in favor of the convent.

Shortly after this event, the prior and convent of Wenlock being disturbed in the possession of the advowson, resigned it to the Bishop of Winchester; in which see it continued till the episcopacy of John de Pontisserâ; who at the request of Edward I. appropriated the church to the convent of Breamore. At the dissolution it was granted to Henry Courtney, Marquis of Exeter; but on his attainder, was given to Trinity College, Cambridge.†

* Sir Richard Worsley's Hist. p. 191 to p. 274.

† Year-tenths of this vicarage are 2l. 8s. It is dedicated to St. Mary.

The

The church of Yaverland was built towards the clofe of the thirteenth century, probably by one of the Ruffel family. It pays a fmall penfion to the mother church of Brading. It is called a chapel in Cardinal Beaufort's valuation, and exempted from taxation on account of its inability.*

The chapel at Shanklin is annexed to Bonchurch. The inhabitants of this parifh, however, bury their dead in that of Brading, and pay an annual penfion of ten fhillings to the Rector of Brading, as an acknowledgment for the fame. The chapel was built and endowed by one of the Lifle family.†

The parifh church of St. Boniface, or Bonchurch, as it is commonly called, was built in the early Anglo-Norman times; but when, is uncertain.‡

* Patron of this rectory is the Rev. Mr. Wright; the valuation in the King's books, 6l. 6. 10½; and its year-tenths, 12s. 8¾.

† The patrons of this vicarage are ―― Hill, Efq. and Mr. Popham.

‡ Patrons, ―― Hill, Efq. and Mr. Popham; year-tenths, 2s. 8½.

The church of New-church is a very ancient fabric, built prior to the general Domesday survey; William Fitz-Osborne on receiving the Isle of Wight, presented this church, and five others, to the abbey of Lyra in Normandy, which he founded. It continued part of the possessions of that monastery, till the duchy of Normandy was lost to England, when it was given to Beaulieu Abbey in the New Forest.‡

The parish of New-church includes within it the village of Ryde, where there is a chapel, built by Thomas Player, Esq. in 1719; who charged the manor with an annual rent of ten pounds, payable to the Vicar of New-church, to officiate therein, or provide a minister.*

The church of Whitwell is properly a chapel belonging to Godshill; but having separate parochial rates, it is deemed a distinct

‡ This is a rectory; church dedicated to St. John the Baptist; united to Carisbrook.

* Adjoining this parish is that of St. Lawrence, the church of which is the smallest in the island. It is a rectory; patron Sir R. Worsley, Bart.

parish.

parish. The chapel of St. Radegund, which is now the chancel of the church, was built and endowed by De Estur, Lord of Gatcombe. The Rector of Gatcombe receives the rent of the lands with which the chantry was endowed, for which he ought to officiate in the church at certain times during the year.†

The parish church of Niton, formerly Niweton, and now commonly Crab-Niton, was one of the churches given by William Fitz-Osborne to his abbey of Lyra. It came to the crown at the dissolution, and was presented by Charles I. (with five other churches in Hampshire) to Queen's College, Oxford, in exchange for their plate.*

Godshill church is an ancient Saxon edifice, and was one of the churches bestowed by William Fitz-Osborne on the abbey of Lyra. It afterwards became the property of Sheene Convent in Surry; and is now jointly vested

† This is a vicarage; patrons, Queen's Coll. Oxford.

* It is a rectory; dedicated to St. John Baptist; in King's books 20l. 7. 1; year-tenth 2l. 0. 8½.

in Queen's College, Oxford; and the Worſley family.*

The pariſh church of Arreton was included in the ſix churches given by William Fitz-Oſborne to the abbey of Lyra. Afterwards Baldwin de Redvers beſtowed the manor of Arreton together with its church, on his new foundation, Quarr Abbey; in which they remained till the diſſolution.†

The pariſh church of Binſtead was probably built by one of the Biſhops of Wincheſter, having always belonged to that ſee, and paid an annual penſion of two ſhillings to the ſacriſt of the monaſtery there. It is ſubjected to the rector of Calbourn, who formerly claimed archidiaconal juriſdiction over Binſtead and Brixton.‡

The ſmall pariſh of Wootton was taken out of Whippingham pariſh in the reign of Henry

* The church is dedicated to All Saints; its year-tenths are 3l. 15. 9. It is a vicarage.

† This church is dedicated to St. George; patron, John Fleming, Eſq. year-tenths, 2l. 2.—It is a vicarage.

‡ Binſtead is a rectory dedicated to the Holy Croſs; patron, Biſhop of Wincheſter. Year-tenths, 2s. 8½.

III.

III. when Walter de Infulâ built the chapel, and endowed it with glebe, arable, pasture, and wood-lands; adding, at the same time, certain other tithes. This church was afterwards consumed by fire, when the one now standing was erected upon the same site. Adjoining to the original church, was a chapel dedicated to St. Edmund the King, which had an independent endowment, and a chaplain distinct from the rector of the church.*

The church of Northwood is a chapel of ease to Carisbrook, but, since the reign of Henry VIII. has enjoyed all parochial privileges, and is exempted from contributing to the repairs of the mother church. When the priory of Carisbrook obtained the rectory, and endowed the vicarage, the tithes of Northwood, both great and small, were assigned to the vicar. The

* Wootton is a rectory dedicated to St. Edmund.— Patron, Rev. Mr. Walton; valuation in King's books, 7l. 16. 0½; Year-tenths, 15s. 7¼. Adjoining to this parish is that of Whippingham; it is a rectory; patron, the King. Val. King's books, 19l. 1. 5½. Year-tenths, 1l. 18. 1¾.

Vicar

Vicar of Carisbrook is Rector of Northwood.†

Northwood parish includes West Cowes, the chapel of which place was erected in 1657, consecrated in 1662, and endowed in 1671 by Mr. Richard Stephens, with five pounds per annum for ever. It was farther endowed in the year 1679, by Bishop Morley, with twenty pounds per annum; provided the inhabitants paid the minister (who is always appointed by them) an additional forty pounds per annum; otherwise the said endowment to be forfeited for ever.

Newport church is supposed to have been erected towards the latter end of Henry the Second's reign. The inhabitants, however, had no burial-place here till the time of Queen Elizabeth, when they were indebted to one of the heaviest of God's visitations, for the privilege of interment.*

† The church is dedicated to St. John the Baptist.

* The plague was so heavy at Newport, that the burial-place of Carisbrook, the mother church, was not sufficiently large to receive the number of the dead.

Carisbrook being the mother church, the appointment of the curate of Newport is *strictly* in the vicar of that parish. But as the stipend paid to the officiating minister arises from a rate levied on the town's-people, they seem, in justice, entitled to have their inclination consulted in the appointment. The present incumbent, however, appears not to be of this opinion; and has actually given a nomination contrary to the wishes of the parish. The consequence of this is an universal discontent, extremely prejudicial to the interests of religion; for the larger part of the congregation, disgusted at having a minister forced upon them, contrary to their choice, have, for some time past, discontinued their attendance on divine worship. Whether the pertinacity of the curate in holding the appointment under these circumstances, or that of the congregation in continuing to testify their disgust in this manner, be most blamable, must be left for others to determine.

St. Nicholas chapel, in Carisbrook castle, was built either by William Fitz-Osborne, or his son

Roger,

Roger, Earl of Hereford; and given by Baldwin de Redvers to Quarr Abbey, together with its lands. The parish of St. Nicholas has no other place of worship than this chapel, at which, for many years, no service has been performed; hence its little living is a *sinecure*, in the gift of the Governor of the Isle of Wight. The crown pays for this chapel three pounds a year to the Vicar of Carisbrook, as an acknowledgment to the mother church.*

The parish church of Carisbrook is a pile of great antiquity, erected before the Domesday survey, as appears by its being mentioned therein, and called The Church of the Manor. It was formerly of much greater extent than it is at present; Sir Francis Walsingham (in the reign of Elizabeth) having robbed it of its chancel. He was led to do this by a parsimony not very justifiable; for, having the lease of the priory, and by that being obligated to repair this part of the edifice, he avoided the expence soon after he became the lessee, by persuading

* It is a vicarage.—Year-tenths, 14s.

the

the parishioners that the body of the church would be sufficiently large for them. To his persuasions, he added the magic of one hundred marks, and by the united force of both, the devoted chancel fell.*

"It does not appear when Gatcombe church was erected. The manor, however, is as old as Edward the Confessor's time; to which the patronage of the church was always annexed. The chantry called *Cantaria Manerii de Gatcombe,* was at Whitwell, and dedicated to St. Radigund. The land adjoining to that chapel, which was the endowment of the chantry, is esteemed to be in the parish of Gatcombe, and pays a pension to it as the mother church. The Vicar of Godshill officiates in the chapel of Whitwell, where the Rector of Gatcombe is bound to assist him; but the distance rendering it inconvenient for him to discharge that duty, he

---

* This is a vicarage; patron, Queen's Coll. Oxford; valuation in King's books, 23l. 8. 1½. year-tenths, 2l. 6s. 9¼. Church dedicated to St. Mary.

pays

pays four nobles per annum to the Vicar of Godſhill to perform the whole.†

The church of Kingſton (which is the ſmalleſt pariſh in the iſland) was built by one of the Kingſton family, who long poſſeſſed the manor. They alſo appear, by the regiſters of the Biſhops of Wincheſter, to have enjoyed the preſentation to it.*

Chale church was built by Hugh Vernun, in the reign of Henry I. and dedicated to St. Andrew. This pariſh being originally included in that of Cariſbrook, the prieſt of the latter claimed the new church of Chale as ſoon as it was erected; a claim which the founder endeavoured to diſprove. To terminate, however, all animoſities, Hugh Vernun agreed to aſſign to the church of Cariſbrook a moiety of the glebe land, and tithes of burials

† This is a rectory; patron, Edward Meux Worſley, Eſq. valuation in King's books, 25l. 18. 9. year-tenths, 2l. 11. 1¼.

* It is a rectory; patron, —— Worſley, Eſq. val. in King's books, 5l. 6. 8. year-tenths, 10s. 8.

and

and oblations, excepting thofe of his own houfe, which he referved entire, for maintaining the fervice and repairs of the church of Chale. The Parfon of Chale, alfo, was to perform the whole fervice of his church; and on thefe confiderations, the Prieft of Carifbrook teftified his confent to the new church having a cemetery; an agreement which the Bifhop of Winchefter, William Gifford, confirmed under his anathema.§

The church of Shorwell, (formerly a chapel) was built fhortly after the foundation of Carifbrook priory; and confirmed to it by the charter of William de Vernun. It was included in the parifh of Carifbrook till the reign of Edward III. when the inconvenience of carrying its dead to be buried fuch a diftance, occafioned its feparation from that parifh, and having parochial rights of its own.‡

§ It is a rectory; patron, Sir R. Worfley, Bart. val. in King's books, 14l. 3. 11¼. year-tenths, 1l. 8. 4¾.

‡ Shorwell is a rectory; valuation in King's books, 20l. 0. 2½. year-tenths, 2l. 0. 0¾. dedicated to St. Peter.

The parish of Brixton was taken out of that of Calbourn by one of the Bishops of Winchester, who built its church, and endowed it with parochial privileges. The former rectory anciently claimed archidiaconal jurisdiction over that of Brixton, to which the rectors of the latter refusing to submit, the contest rose to actual violence.* The claim, however, was probably accommodated by the bishop, the patron of both churches.†

Motteston church was built in the twelfth century. In the fourteenth, we find it, together with the manor, in the possession of the Langford family; for Dionysia, widow of Sir John de Langford, presented to it in 1364. Edward Cheke, Esq. presented to it in 1374;

---

* There was anciently a dean of this island, to superintend ecclesiastical affairs; we find also, by the registers of Winchester, that William of Wykeham substituted a suffragan bishop here, as was afterwards done by Henry VIII.

† Brixton is a rectory; patron, Bishop of Winchester; val. in King's books, 32l. 3. 4. year-tenths, 3l. 4. 4. Church dedicated to St. Mary.

and

and with his defcendents it continued for above three centuries.*

Calbourn church appears to have had thirty fhillings from the manor of that name, in the time of Edward the Confeffor; a circumftance which proves its remote antiquity. The advowfon of it, remained in the fee of Winchefter till the time of Edward I. who in the twelfth year of his reign, deprived the bifhop of that diocefe (in confequence of a perfonal pique,) both of the church and manor of Calbourn. They were however afterwards returned, in confequence of a heavy fine paid by the bifhop to Edward.‡

There is a chapel at Newtown, a manor within this parifh, which belongs to Calbourn church; and the glebe with which it is endowed, is enjoyed by the rector. In the furvey of the

* It is a rectory; valuation in King's books, 11l. 16. 3d. year-tenths, 1l. 3. 7¼. Dedicated to St. Peter and St. Paul.

‡ It is a rectory; patron, Bifhop of Winchefter; valuation in King's books, 19l. 17. 8¼; year-tenths, 1l. 19. 9. Dedicated to All Saints.

ifland

island taken in the reign of Elizabeth, the Parson of Calbourn is said to hold a grant of forty acres, called Magdalen's land, belonging to the chapel of Newtown, for which land he provided a reader for the chapel.

The church of Shalfleet is mentioned in the Domesday survey, and probably was built shortly before that general census. Edward III. granted it to William Montecute, Earl of Salisbury; who gave it to his new-founded abbey of Bisham in Berkshire. The impropriation, after the dissolution of the monasteries, was purchased by Lord Chief Justice Fleming, and devised by him to a younger branch of his family. It is now in the crown.*

It is not known at what period the church of Brook was erected. Some years since a dispute occurred relative to the patronage of it, between St. John's College, Cambridge, which claimed it as a chapel belonging to Freshwater, and the Bowerman family, who possessed the manor of Brook. The cause was tried, and determined in

* Shalfleet is a vicarage; year-tenths, 1l. 17. 2¼.

favor

favor of the latter; which family has ever since presented to it.*

The church of Thorley was probably built by Amicia, Countess of Devon, who gave it to the priory of Christchurch, in Hampshire. where it remained till the dissolution. It was then exchanged (with other estates of the priory) with Thomas Hopson, Esquire, in 1546, for his manor of Marybone in Middlesex.†

The present church of Yarmouth was built in the thirty-fifth year of Henry VIII. This is not, however, its original one. In the thirteenth century, a small chapel was erected at the East end of the present town, which the French, in one of their descents on the island, destroyed. A second place of worship was then built at the Western extremity, and this too fell a sacrifice to the same people, in a visit which they made in the reign of Henry VIII. A third time the

* It is a rectory; year-tenths, 3s. 10¼. Dedicated to St. Mary.

† It is a vicarage; year-tenths, 13s. 10¼. Dedicated to St. Swithin.

inhabitants

inhabitants rebuilt their church, and placed it in the middle of the town, where it at present stands. The endowment of this church being extremely small, it was augmented by the bounty of Queen Anne; to which was added a sum of money given by Colonel Henry Holmes, for that purpose.*

The church of Freshwater was given by William Fitz-Osborne to his abbey of Lyra; where it continued till the alien monasteries were seized on by the crown. It was afterwards repeatedly granted to the captains of the island for the time being; but at length given to St. John's College, Cambridge, where it now remains.†

* It is a rectory; patron, the King. Dedicated to St. James.

† It is a rectory; valuation, King's books, 19l. 8. 4. year-tenths, 1l. 18. 10. Dedicated to All Saints.

THE

CIVIL HISTORY

OF THE

ISLE OF WIGHT.

CHAP. I.

OF THE BOROUGHS OF NEWPORT, NEWTOWN, AND YARMOUTH.

THE Isle of Wight sends to the House of Commons, six members; two for Newport, two for Newtown, and the same number for Yarmouth.

Of these boroughs, Newport and Yarmouth returned representatives to parliament as early as the twenty-third year of Edward I. a period, according to antiquaries, when the representatives of the commons were first legally convened.*

S. The

* Willis's Not. Parl. Preface.

The incorporation of Newport by charter took place in the firſt year of James I. when the bailiff and burgeſſes of the place were conſtituted a body politic; the corporation to conſiſt of a mayor, and twenty-four burgeſſes. By this charter, the mayor, recorder, or his deputy, with two of the burgeſſes, are impowered to hold a court on every Friday, for the trial of all ſmall cauſes ariſing within the borough; to take recognizances of debts according to the ſtatutes merchant, and of the ſtaple; and to have a gaol for the reception of ſuch perſons as they ſhould commit for debts, felonies, or other offences.

Charles II. in the thirteenth year of his reign, granted another charter to Newport; in which the ſtyle of the corporation is altered from its original one, to that of *Mayor, Aldermen,* and *Burgeſſes.* By this charter, the mayor is to be choſen from among the aldermen, who are twelve in number; theſe are to be choſen out of the chief burgeſſes, by the mayor and aldermen; and the mayor is to be ſworn into

into his office before the governor of the island or his steward.* Amongst other privileges granted or confirmed by this charter, it is mentioned, that the mayor, aldermen, and chief burgesses are exempted from serving on juries at the assizes, or general quarter sessions.

From the twenty-third of Edward I. to the twenty-seventh year of Elizabeth, Newport does not appear to have sent any representatives to parliament; but since the latter period, its returns of two members to each parliament have been very regular.

Newport was constituted a *borough* almost as soon as it came into the possession of the De Redvers family; Richard, the son of the first grantee, bestowing on its inhabitants those various liberties which in early days formed a borough.† These liberties consisted of a permission

---

* This ceremony is now performed in the old chapel of St. Nicholas, in Carisbrook castle.

† It is difficult to ascertain precisely, the origin of burghs in this kingdom; though we find them mentioned in the laws of *Ina* King of the West Saxons, which

miffion to trade under the protection of the lord of the demefne : a right of exacting a toll for all goods brought to be difpofed of within the limits of the borough : a privilege of having a market, and holding fairs in the fame; and various others of the like nature : liberties which were generally, either purchafed originally of the lord by thofe on whom they were conferred, or paid for, by a regular annual rent levied on every burgefs.*

A fecond

which gives them an antiquity of nearly eleven hundred years. Among the municipal conftitutions of this wife monarch, for the internal peace and government of his kingdom, we find an ordinance to this effect; that, " whoever fhall be guilty of a violation of the peace in a *borough* under the protection of the king or bifhop, he fhall pay one hundred and twenty fhillings." Leges Inæ apud Lambarde Archaionom. p. ix. c. 46. Vide my " Topographical Remarks relating to Hampfhire." Blamire, 1792, vol. II. p. 51.

* Boroughs, we have feen in the laft note, were of Saxon origin. They were intended for the promotion of induftry and commerce; and their inhabitants were encouraged to exertion by particular privileges, immunities, and laws. Here markets were eftablifhed; imports and exports of various merchandife carried on,

under

A second charter of immunities and privileges
was granted by Isabella de Fortibus, in the
thirteenth century, to the burgesses of Newport;
by which she invests them with the power of
taking toll *throughout the whole island*, in all villages and roads; on the sea, and in the har-

under the *Prepositus Burghi*, or bailiff of the borough,
appointed by the prince or lord of the fee to reside in
the place, and gather the tolls, duties, and impositions,
arising from the trade of it. Notwithstanding, however,
the various regulations thus made in favor of those who
inhabited boroughs, their state, for the most part, in the
Saxon times, seems to have been nothing more than a
certain qualified slavery. Repeated notices occur in
Domesday book, of towns whose burgesses were confined
to a residence on the spot where they traded; who were
so completely under the dominion of their lord, that they
could not do homage to, nor receive protection from any
other superior. In this state, it is probable, the boroughs
remained till the Anglo-Norman kings took possession of
the English crown; who, finding that commerce was
cramped by the restrictions under which the burgesses
labored, relaxed by degrees the servile ties, and remitted
the numerous imposts that had arisen in the Saxon times;
granting them liberty of person, and accepting, in lieu of
the duties formerly received, a fixed redditus, called a
fee-farm rent, which was proportioned to the amount of the
original impositions. At the same time also we may look
for the origin of *chartered corporations*.—Topog. Remarks,
vol. II. p. 54.

bour;*

bour;* in fairs, and at markets; in all places, and on all commodities. She further grants, an exemption to the burgeffes from attending the hundred and county courts; a privilege of depafturing their cattle in her foreft of Parkhurft; a power of trying all pleas arifing within the borough, and fixing the quantum of fines on conviction; and a liberty of retaining and dividing amongft themfelves all fuch fines as fhould fo arife. All which immunities and privileges were to be held by the faid burgeffes, in confideration of their paying to her and her heirs, eighteen marks, annually; and to the prior and monks of Carifbrook, two marks, annually.† This charter was confirmed by Edward III. Richard II. Henry VII. Edward IV. Henry VIII. Edward VI. and Queen Elizabeth; fome of whom, particularly Edward IV. added other grants and privileges to the borough, fuch as the

* This is the foundation of a duty even now paid at Cowes, by all fhips which caft anchor in that road.

† Carta Ifabellæ Corn. Alb. Sir R. Worfley's Append. No. XXI.

for-

forfeitures of outlaws, felons, and fuicides, within the borough; and the petty cuftoms of any port or creek in the ifland.

This town has given title to four *earls*: Lord Mountjoy Blount, natural fon of the Earl of Devonfhire, created by Charles I. Baron of Thurflfton, and Earl of Newport. He died in the year 1665, and his three fons fucceffively enjoyed the title. On the deceafe of Henry, the laft furviving one, unmarried, it became extinct. Lord Windfor was alfo *Baron* Newport in Queen Anne's reign.

The borough of Newtown (which changed its ancient name of Francheville, on being rebuilt when burnt by the French in the reign of Richard II.) is a prefcriptive borough, and firft fent members to the fenate in the twenty-feventh year of Queen Elizabeth. It was formerly a place of confiderable confequence; and traces of its magnitude are ftill difcernible in four lanes, which interfect each other at right angles, and are faid, formerly to have been covered with houfes.

The

The first liberties and franchises granted to the burgesses of Newtown are contained in a charter of Aymer, Bishop of Winchester, lord of the place; who invests his town of Francheville, with all such immunities and privileges as were enjoyed by the inhabitants of Taunton, Alesford, and Farnham. This charter bears date at Swanifton: and afterwards received the several confirmations of Edward II. Edward IV. and Queen Elizabeth. Edward II. also granted to the burgesses of Newtown, a charter in the eleventh year of his reign; in which is bestowed the liberty of a *market* to be holden on the Wednesday in every week; and of a fair annually, on the feast of St. Mary Magdalene, on the eve preceding, and on the day following.

The elective franchise in this borough was determined by the House of Commons in 1729, to be confined to the mayor and burgesses, having borough lands. Previous to this final adjustment of the right, perpetual contests arose relative to the exertion of it. The most ancient books of the corporation prove, that the qualifications fication of a burgefs was formerly the holding of a *borough land*, paying rent to the mayor and chief burgeffes; but in the time of Charles II. the right of voting was confined to the burgeffes alone, and the number of thefe limited to twelve. This limitation however was pronounced illegal by the corporation, in the reign of William III. which met on the twentieth day of September, 1698, and came to the following refolutions:

" At this affembly, upon examining the ancient records of the faid corporation, (Newtown, alias Francheville) and taking the depofitions on oath of James Overy; as alfo upon the averment of fome of the chief burgéffes there, then prefent; it is refolved, that the reftraint of the chief bur-, geffes of this corporation, to the number of twelve, or any lefs number than are freeholders of borough lands is againft law, and contrary to the ancient ufage of this corporation."

" Alfo 'tis ordered and agreed; that whofoever fhall prove himfelf to be a freeholder, of any borough land in fee, either by the rent-roll now produced in this affembly, bearing date and

beginning

beginning in the year of our Lord 1685, (whereof a true copy shall be kept by the mayor for the time being) or otherwise effectually in law, shall upon demand, be sworn a chief burgess."

This meeting had been convened in consequence of an agreement entered into during the preceding year, between Lord Cutts, the then governor, and the principal gentlemen in the island; the object of which was, to restore that harmony, good fellowship and neighbourhood of the district, that had been mightily interrupted by constant disputes relative to the right of voting in the three corporations of Newport, Newtown, and Yarmouth. In these articles of agreement it was stipulated, that the governor should call a hall at Newtown, examine witnesses concerning the ancient method of choosing members to serve in parliament for that corporation, and effectually restore the said corporation, and all who have a just pretence to be members of it, to their ancient rights of burgage-tenure: provided always, that the said governor be first put in possession of a qualifying burgage-tenure, sufficient

ficient to enable him to be a member and elector of the said corporation: he paying for the same.

The meeting was called, and the regulations above detailed entered into at it.*

In the course of a few years, however, after this adjustment, the right of voting became again the occasion of controversy. The corporation, on inspecting the old books of the borough, discovered that the arrangement of 1698 was contrary to the ancient usage; the minutes of that meeting were therefore erased from the town-book, and those who enjoyed a *freehold in a borough land* were once more

---

* The Corporation at that time consisted of,
John, Lord Cutts, Mayor.
Joseph Dudley, Esq. Deputy-Mayor.

Henry Dore	James Worsley, Esq.
Col. David Urry	Col. Richard Holmes
Mr. John Chiverton	Mr. Edward Hayles
Major Henry Holmes	Sir Rob. Worsley, Bart.
Mr. John Philips	William Stephen, Esq.
Mr. David Urry	William Bowerman, Esq.
John Leigh, Esq.	

invested

invested with a right of voting for a reprefentative for Newtown.

We have feen that this regulation was reverfed by the Houfe of Commons in 1729, which lodged the privilege in the *mayor and burgeffes having borough lands*.

The borough of Yarmouth fent its reprefentatives to the parliament convened in the twenty-third of Edward I. It had a fecond fummons in the twenty-feventh of Queen Elizabeth, from which period its returns of two members to the Britifh fenate have been very regular.

Its firft charter appears to have been granted by Baldwin de Redvers, Earl of Devon, brother of Ifabella de Fortibus; which comprized nearly the fame rights or privileges as the grants to Newport and Newtown. James I, who reincorporated a multitude of the boroughs, formed this alfo into a regular corporation, by a charter bearing date the firft of September, in the feventh year of his reign, which in effect is as follows:

" Whereas

"Whereas the borough of Eremuth, alias Yarmouth, in the Ifle of Wight, is an ancient borough, and the mayor and burgeffes have prefcribed to have and ufe diverfe liberties and privileges, which they claim alfo under colour of charters of confirmation from feveral kings and queens of this realm, confirming an ancient grant made to this borough by Baldwin de Redvers, fome time lord of this ifle; viz. the charter of confirmation under the great feal, in the eighth year of the reign of King Edward I. a like charter granted in the eighteenth of Henry VI. another charter of the fixth of Edward IV. and another charter of the fecond of Elizabeth: And whereas the faid mayor and burgeffes, and their predeceffors, have always paid to the king and his predeceffors, for the faid privileges, immunities, and liberties, the fee-farm of twenty fhillings yearly; and whereas it appears by the records in the Remembrancer's office in the Exchequer, in the fecond year of Richard II. that the town of Yarmouth was entirely burned by the enemy, and its inhabitants greatly impoverifhed;

poverished; and whereas the said town lies near to a good harbour for shipping, and, for that reason, King Henry VIII. caused a castle to be built, since which the town is better inhabited than before; and it is to be hoped that it will yet be more filled with people, for increasing the strength of the island, and guarding the said castle, if his majesty would vouchsafe to regrant them their liberties and immunities: that the said mayor and burgesses, esteeming the charters before-mentioned insufficient to authorize them in the using and enjoying the said liberties and immunities, have petitioned the king, to make, confirm, and new create them a body politic and corporate, with such franchises as shall be by the king thought expedient: that the king therefore being willing to settle the rules for the government of the said borough and the people there, declares it to be a free borough; and that they shall be a body politic and corporate, by the name of mayor and burgesses of Yarmouth, in the Isle of Wight, with capacity to purchase, &c. to grant, &c. to plead or to be impleaded, and to

have

have a common seal; that there shall be twelve
chief burgesses to be the common council of the
borough; that, out of these, one shall be chosen
mayor of the borough; that they shall have
power to make laws, statutes, and orders, for the
government of the borough and its officers; that
the burgesses of the said borough shall continue
for life, excepting any of them shall be removed
for reasonable cause; and on the death or
removal of a chief burgess, the mayor and major
part of the burgesses then living shall elect another
in his place, who shall be sworn before the
mayor and major part of the chief burgesses;
that the mayor and steward of the borough shall
hold the courts of the said borough; that they
shall hold a view of frank pledge of all inhabiting and resident in the said borough,
and to redress abuses in the same; the
mayor and burgesses are empowered to elect and
constitute a steward, a common clerk, and a
sergeant at mace, to continue during the pleasure
of the mayor and burgesses; that the mayor and
burgesses shall have all the fines, forfeitures, and
profits

profits of the courts, which they shall have power to levy, by their own officers by distress: they have also a grant of strays, and the goods of felons, within the limits of the borough: a market is granted to the town, to be kept every Wednesday; and a fair to be held yearly, viz. on St. James's day, the eve before, and the day after, together with a court of pie-powder, &c. with all the profits and emoluments belonging to such markets, fairs, and courts: a special licence and authority are given to the mayor and burgesses, to purchase and hold to them and burgesses for ever any manors, lands, &c. not holden of the king *in capite,* or by knight's service, not exceeding the value of twenty pounds per annum, the statute of mortmain notwithstanding; and licence is also given for any person, &c. to grant and alien to the said mayor and burgesses, under the like restriction, all liberties, privileges, franchises, and immunities, which the borough has held and enjoyed, by reason or colour of grants by the king or any of his predecessors, or by any other persons made heretofore, are confirmed;

saving

saving and reserving out of this grant, the castle of Yarmouth, its ditches, trenches, and limits, wherein the said mayor and burgesses have no power or authority to enter: they are to pay the fee-farm of *twenty shillings* yearly, at the feast of St. Michael; a clause is added to indemnify them from all prosecutions for any liberties or franchises used, had, or usurped by them, before the date of this charter, and no fine is to be paid to the Hanaper office for it.*

Yarmouth had the honor of entertaining Charles II. in the year 1671. He spent a short time in this town, at a house built entirely for his accommodation, by Sir Robert Holmes; it has many years since been converted into an inn; and, blending the memorial of its having lodged a royal visitor, with a compliment to the reigning family, is now called the George. The monarch in this excursion landed at Gurnard's Bay, and in his way to Yarmouth passed through the forest of Parkhurst, over a road which Sir Robert Holmes had formed on purpose to accommodate him.

* Sir Richard Worsley's Hist. p. 159.

The circumstances of this visit are tenaciously remembered by the inhabitants of the island, whose beautiful residence has had the pleasure of receiving only three of its monarchs since the conquest,—King John, Henry VIII. and Charles II.

CHAP. II.

OF THE LORDS OF THE ISLAND; THEIR POWER, RIGHTS, AND FRANCHISES; AND OF THE KNIGHTON COURT.

THE barons of the feudal ages enjoyed on their own demesnes an authority almost regal. The lords of the Isle of Wight, by the grant of Henry I. became possessed of all those rights in the amplest degree, with which the higher fees were endowed. They had their own courts of judicature for the trial of all offences, save those of treason and murder. They nominated their own bailiffs, constables, and all other petty officers. They executed the office of coroner throughout the whole island. They had the return of all the king's writs. They possessed a chace, now called

Parkhurst

Parkhurst Forest; a fence-mouth there, and in other places; and a free warren on the East side of the river Medina; together with wrecks, waifs, and strays. The tenants of the island were chargeable in aid to them alone;† and held their lands as of the castle of Carisbrooke. By the regulations of their tenure, the tenants were bound to assist (distinct from their customary aids) in the charge of making the eldest son of the lord a knight; of marrying his daughter; and of paying the ransom for his liberation should he be made a prisoner. They were also obligated to defend the castle of Carisbrooke for forty days, at their own costs and charges, whenever it might be attacked; and to attend the lord both on his coming to the island, and departing from it. Moreover, the lord enjoyed the right of wardship over the whole island; a right which placed every heir that was a minor under his

† They paid no regular annual tax to the lord; but as often as the king levied a scutage upon him for the island, so often his feudatories contributed each his settled proportion towards the payment of it.

protection;

protection; that conferred on him the rents and profits of the estate during the minority, and enabled him to give the ward in marriage to whomsoever he pleased.

Many are the traces of this feudal government, which subsist to the present day, both in the Isle of Wight, and every other part of the kingdom; one remnant, however, deserves particular mention, as it formerly constituted one of the greatest privileges which the lord of this district enjoyed.

This is the *Knight's Court*, or *Knighton Court*, as it is now called, or the *Curia Militum*, as it was anciently stiled. It received this appellation from the circumstance of those who held a knight's, or part of a knight's fee in capite, being the judges in this tribunal; where they gave judgment according to the Norman mode of trial, without a jury. This principle of decision, so contrary to the spirit of Anglo-Saxon jurisprudence, leads one to apprehend the Knighten Court had its origin during the period of William Fitz-Osborne's possessing the

Isle

Isle of Wight, who modelled it after the court of judicature in his own country.

In the year 1626 an attempt was made to improve and enlarge the jurifdiction of this court, when the following reprefentation of its form and extent, was tranfmitted to Lord Conway, then governor of the ifland.

Knighten Court.

" 1. It hath been always kept by the captain's fteward of the ifland, or his fubftitute, by virtue of the captain's patent, and by no other particular patent, for aught we know."

" 2. It hath been always kept in the townhall of Newport, on the Monday every three weeks, unlefs that day happen a feftival day, and then it is adjourned for fix weeks."

" 3. It hath jurifdiction throughout the whole ifland, the corporation of Newport excepted."

" 4. It holdeth plea of all actions of debt and trefpafs, under the value of forty fhillings, and upon replevins granted by the fteward or his fubftitute that keeps the court."

" 5. The

" 5. The procefs in actions of debt and trefpafs, are fummons, attachments, and diftringas, to bring the defendant to appear; which if he do in perfon, he muft confefs the action, or elfe he is condemned by default; if by an attorney, he is admitted one effoine, if he prays it, and the next court muft appear, or be condemned by default. And in actions upon replevins, if the defendant appear not in the three firft courts, he is condemned by default: and in thefe actions upon replevins, no effoine is admitted."

" 6. The pleadings are Englifh bills and anfwers; and if the cafe require, replications and rejoinders."

" 7. All the actions are entered, profecuted, and pleaded, by certain attornies allowed in that court."

" 8. The actions of debt are tried by proof of plaintiff or defendant, or the defendant's wager of law with two hands, if he pray it, and in trefpafs by proof only."

" 9. All the actions are adjudged by the court, without jury; which it will be conceived
will

will be better with jury, as in other courts of record, if the value of actions be increafed."

" 10. The judges are freeholders, which hold of his majefty's caftle of Carifbrooke; whereof there are known to the fteward not above eighteen. The which freeholders, for their better eafe, have been appointed by the captain of the ifle to fit by four or five at a court by turns; but fome being aged and impotent, one under age, fome living out of the ifle, and fome of the reft being negligent of that fervice, there hath been much defect in their attendance; which is to the great prejudice of the court, and hindrance of the people, by delay of trials."

" Therefore, under favor, we conceive, that a certain form of election of a certain number of judges, of other fufficient men of the country, fhall be added; and a ftrict order taken for their due attendance will be very neceffary, efpecially if the value of actions be raifed: and that if there be not an efpecial reftraint of removing actions in that court triable from thence

thence into higher courts, that court will do little more good than it doth already."

This statement being delivered to the privy council, orders were immediately issued by the Lord Treasurer, Viscount Grandison, to the attorney-general, to prepare forthwith a grant for extending the jurisdiction of the Knighten Court, " to all cases whatsoever, civil or criminal, under the value of twenty pounds, provided that the same extend not to the life, member, or freehold of any of the inhabitants.". Notwithstanding this mandate, however, the business was not proceeded in; and the jurisdiction of the Knighten Court, and mode of decision therein, continue the same as before.†

† Sir R. Worsley's Hist. p. 81. et infra.

CHAP. III.

OF THE WARDENS, CAPTAINS, AND GOVERNORS OF THE ISLAND.

As soon as the Isle of Wight became the property of the crown, Edward I. appointed a warden to regulate its concerns.

Indeed, during its continuance in the De Redvers family, the reigning monarch had twice, when the owner was a minor, and his property therefore (according to the feudal system) became temporarily vested in the crown, appointed a warden, who exercised the rights of the lord, during the nonage of the heir. The first instance of this, happened in the first of Henry III. when Walleran de Ties received

ceived the cuſtody of the iſland in the minority of Baldwin the third, grandſon of William de Vernon. The ſecond took place in the thirteenth of Henry III. when Savery de Mauleon, or de Malo Leone, was appointed to the office in the minority of Baldwin the fourth.

In the year 1293, Edward I. conſtituted John Fitz-Thomas warden of the iſland; who enjoyed alſo the ſtewardſhip of New Foreſt.

Richard de Affeton appears to have held this office in the twenty-ſecond year of Edward I. And in the enſuing year, the Biſhop of Winchester, and Adam de Gordon, were included with him in another commiſſion for the ſame appointment. A record of the ſame year ſhews that William Ruſſel alſo was warden at this time.

Sir John Liſle of Wootton was appointed to the wardenſhip of the iſland in the thirtieth of Edward I. and made captain of Cariſbrooke Caſtle. On the acceſſion of Edward II. he was ſuperſeded, and his brother appointed in his ſtead; but the latter being murdered by one Robert Urry, in the third of Edward II. Sir John Lisle was restored to his dignity and office.

Sir Henry Ties was appointed warden under Prince Edward, in 1321; the same person probably who was beheaded in the ensuing year, for being concerned in rebellion with Thomas, Earl of Lancaster, who also lost his head.

In the eighteenth of Edward II. John de la Huse and John Lisle were wardens of the island. Nicholas de la Felde occurs as *custos* during the same year.

In the ninth of Edward III. 1336, John de Langford of Chale, was warden of the island, and captain of Carisbrooke Castle.

In the eleventh of the same king, Theobald Russel occurs as captain general of the island.

The abbot of Quarr was appointed warden of the island in 1340; to whom was directed a writ to act in the capacity of a general officer, by arraying men, supplying arms, and erecting beacons.

Three commissioners were *elected by the inhabitants* of the island, to act as wardens, in 1341;

Sir

Sir Bartholomew Lisle, John de Langford Lord of Chale, and Sir Theobald Ruffel Lord of Yaverland.

In 1353, three other wardens are found acting at one time; Bartholomew Lisle, John de Kingston, and Henry Romyn.

John de Gatesden received a commission, as warden of the island, to array the inhabitants, in the year 1353.

In 1360, the abbot of Quarr, Theobald de Gorges, and William Dale, were appointed wardens.

In 1377, the first of Richard II. the gallant Sir Hugh Tyrril, who, as we have before seen, defended the castle of Carisbrooke against the French, was constable of that fortress.

In the seventeenth year of Henry VI. Humphrey, Duke of Gloucester, son of Henry IV. succeeded to the lordship of the island, after the decease of the Duchess of York, (grantee of it under the crown). He died in the twenty-fifth of Henry VI. and on his decease, that king immediately appointed Henry Trenchard

to the office of conftable of the caftle of Carifbrooke, with a falary of twenty pounds per
annum; ten pounds as keeper of the foreft of
Parkhurft; and four-pence per day for the
pay of the porter of the caftle.

In the reign of Henry VI. the lordfhip of the
ifland was conferred on Richard, Duke of York;
who appointed one John Newport his lieutenant
and fteward. The behaviour of this deputy was
fo oppreffive, that Richard removed him from
the office, and appointed John Bruin in his ftead.

In 1461, the firft of Edward IV. the captain-
fhip of the ifland was conferred on Sir Geoffry
Gate, for life. He furrendered it, however, in
1467, and it was given to Anthony, Lord Schales,
the uncle of the king.

Early in the year 1483, Sir William Berkley
was made captain of the ifland; and towards
the clofe of it, Sir John Saville was appointed
to the fame office.

Sir Edward Woodville was entrufted with the
command of the ifland at the acceffion of
Henry VII.

In

In the tenth of Henry VII. Sir Reginald Bray received a grant of the ifland, on leafe, with the caftle and honor of Carifbrooke, &c. (late in the poffeffion of George, Duke of Clarence) at the annual rent of three hundred and feven marks. On his death Sir Nicholas Wadham fucceeded him; anceftor to the founder of Wadham College, Oxford.

Early in the third year of Henry VIII. Sir Nicholas Wadham died, and was fucceeded by Sir James Worfley, keeper of the king's wardrobe, and mafter of the robes. He was conftituted captain of the ifland for life, with a falary of fix fhillings and nine-pence per diem for himfelf, two fhillings for his deputy, and fixpence each for thirteen fervants; added to this was a reverfionary grant of the office of conftable of Carifbrooke caftle, when it fhould become vacant, and the command of all the forts in the ifland. He was likewife conftituted keeper of Carifbrooke foreft and park, with a fee of two fhillings per day. He was empowered too, to leafe any of the king's houfes, demefne lands, &c. within the ifland;

to

to return all writs; to execute all proceſſes; to regulate the markets; and take inqueſts as coroner.

In the year of 1538, Richard Worſley, Eſq. ſucceeded his father in the office of captain of the Iſle of Wight. He held it till 1553, when finding himſelf obnoxious to Queen Mary, whoſe principles he diſliked and oppoſed, prudence dictated to him to reſign his appointment; in which he was ſucceeded by Mr. Girling; a man of low extraction, and a favorer of popery. On Mary's death, however, Richard Worſley was reinſtated in his office. In the commiſſion which he received on this occaſion inſtructions were contained, to inſtruct the inhabitants of the iſland in the uſe of harquebuſſes, and to introduce them there; orders which he immediately obeyed.

In 1565 the command of the iſland was beſtowed on Edward Horſey, Eſq. afterwards knighted. His memory is held in ſome eſteem by the ſportſmen of the iſland, who attribute the great plenty of hares, and other game found there at preſent, to the attention beſtowed on them during his government.

Sir

Sir George Carey succeeded Sir Edward Horsey. He appears to have been the first captain of the island who assumed the name of *governor;* a circumstance that gave great disgust to the inhabitants, who conceived the title to be an arbitrary and improper one, in a free country.

Henry, Earl of Southampton, succeeded Sir George Carey in the first year of James I. His patent styles him Captain of all the Isle of Wight; Captain of the castle of Carisbrooke, and all other castles and forts within the said isle; also Constable of the castle of Carisbrooke, Warden of the forest of Parkhurst; Steward, Surveyor, and Receiver of all the lands, woods, revenues, &c. of the crown, within the island. His affability, attention, and hospitality, gave extraordinary satisfaction to the inhabitants, and raised the island to an enviable and flourishing state. He won the affections of the gentry by mixing in their diversions; and twice every week threw off the cumbrous state of the governor at a public bowling-green and ordinary, where the knights and gentlemen met for amufement and relaxation.

This popular nobleman died in December 1625, and was fucceeded by John, Lord Conway; who was afterwards made Secretary of ſtate and Prefident of the council.

On his deceafe in 1631, Richard, Lord Wefton, afterwards created Earl of Portland, was conftituted Captain of the Ifle of Wight; an office which was vacated by his death in 1634.

Jerom, Earl of Portland, fucceeded his father. The parliament, as we have before feen, removed this nobleman in 1642, and appointed in his place Philip, Earl of Pembroke.

In 1647, Colonel Hammond was Governor of the Ifle of Wight, and held it for two years. It was during this interval, that the unfortunate Charles I. took refuge here, vainly flattering himfelf he ſhould find a friend in the governor, as his uncle Doctor Henry Hammond was at that time his confidential chaplain. But the fpirit of fanaticifm, the vice of the times,

and

and the suggestions of interest, prevailed on the colonel to forget the ties of duty, and of gratitude; and to give himself up implicitly to the republican party. Instead therefore of finding a refuge in the island, as he expected, Charles soon after his arrival there, began to feel the restrictions of confinement; which gradually became more severe and ignominious, until he was seized by the army, on the twenty-ninth of November 1648, and conducted to the scaffold that closed his unmerited sufferings.

In 1649, Colonel Sydenham succeeded Hammond in the government of the island. He was brother to the celebrated physician of that name.

In 1660, when Charles was restored to the throne of his ancestors, Thomas, Lord Culpeper, received the government of the island; we have before seen that he rendered himself very unpopular in this office, which he resigned in 1667, and was succeeded by Admiral Sir Robert Holmes, a gallant naval officer. He is styled Governor and Captain of the island, in his patent, and of the castles and forts therein. He died in
1692,

1692, and was interred in a vault in Yarmouth church, where a very elegant marble monument is raifed to his memory.

John, Lord Cutts, one of the moſt gallant ſoldiers of his time, and a great favorite of King William, ſucceeded Sir Robert Holmes in the government of the iſland. He reſided much at Cariſbrooke, where he gave very ſuperb and frequent entertainments. He died in 1707, and was ſucceeded by

Charles, Marquis of Wincheſter, afterwards Duke of Bolton; Warden of the New Foreſt; and Lord Lieutenant of the counties of Southampton and Dorſet. As this nobleman reſided very little in the iſland, it was judged prudent to appoint a lieutenant-governor, under him, by royal commiſſion, with a ſalary of twenty ſhillings per diem; an office that was conferred on Colonel Morgan.

The Duke of Bolton was removed in 1710, and General John Richmond Webb appointed governor in his room. This officer immortalized his name, by defeating with a band of ſeven thouſand thoufand men, upwards of twenty thoufand French, at Wynendale, under the command of General La Motte.

William, Lord Cadogan, afterwards an earl, fucceeded General Webb in 1716. He too was a gallant foldier of the great Duke of Marlborough's fchool; and after the death of that commander, was appointed General and Commander in Chief of His Majefty's Forces, Mafter-general of the Ordnance, and Colonel of the firft regiment of foot guards. On his deceafe, in Auguft 1726,

Charles, Duke of Bolton, was appointed Governor and Vice-admiral; but being removed from his offices in 1733, he was fucceeded by

John, Duke of Montagu; who fcarcely held the office a twelvemonth, and was fucceeded by

John, Lord Vifcount Lymington, (foon after created Earl of Portfmouth) in 1734.

Charles, Duke of Bolton was reinftated in 1742, but foon afterwards refigned his offices, when

John,

John, Earl of Portfmouth, was again made Governor of the Ifle of Wight; this happened the twenty-fecond of February 1745.

Thomas, Lord Holmes, on the death of Lord Portfmouth in 1762, fucceeded to this office; which he enjoyed but a fhort time, dying in July 1764. He was fucceeded by

Hans Stanley, Efq. who was removed in 1766, and

Harry, Duke of Bolton, appointed governor in his room; but owing to a fluctuation in the cabinet, this nobleman was difmiffed from the appointment, and in the year 1770,

The Right Honorable Hans Stanley was again nominated to it. He died in 1780, when the Right Honorable Sir Richard Worfley, Bart. one of his Majefty's moft honorable privy council, fucceeded to the offices of Governor, Vice-admiral, &c. of the Ifle of Wight. In the year 1787, thefe were conferred on

The Right Honorable Thomas Orde, the prefent governor.

THE NATURAL HISTORY

OF THE

ISLE OF WIGHT.

"A man need not to fay, What is this? Wherefore is that? for He hath made all things for their ufes."[*]

"ουτ' εγωγε
Ης γαιης δυναμαι γλυκερωτερον αλλο ιδεσθαι."[†]

CHAP. I.

GENERAL DESCRIPTION OF THE ISLAND; CLIMATE; SOIL; TIMBER; RIVERS; SPRINGS; INHABITANTS; DOWNS; AND CURIOUS PARTICULARS RELATING TO THEM.

THE Ifle of Wight is fituated on the coaft of Hampfhire, nearly midway between the two counties of Dorfet and Suffex. It is feparated from the main land, by a ftrait, or arm of the fea, of unequal breadth; being not more than one mile over at the narroweft part, towards the

[*] Ecclefiafticus. [†] Hom. Odyff.

Western extremity; and nearly seven miles across at the Eastern end. The form of the island is rhomboidal; measuring twenty-two miles and an half from the Eastern to the Western angle; and thirteen miles from the Northern to the Southern one: its superficial contents may be computed at one hundred and five thousand acres. It is divided into two Hundreds, called East and West Medine; and contains thirty parishes. Its inhabitants we may estimate at eighteen thousand seven hundred. The face of the country is in general very beautiful, as it possesses all those ingredients, which, properly combined, form *picturesque scenery;* wood, rocks, swelling hills, winding rivers, and rich vales.

The *climate* is pleasant and salubrious, highly favorable to vegetation, which is here generally forwarder than in any other parts of England, if we except the Southern coast of Cornwall. The profusion of myrtles to be seen, for the production of which it has been long famous, evince there is a genial mildness in the air, approaching to the foftnefs of more Southern climates; and there can be no doubt, that fome of the hardier plants of thofe parts might be cultivated here with fuccefs, would the inhabitants bend their attention to the rearing of fuch exotics. It might then literally exhibit the riches of the Italian foil.

" Hîc ver purpureum, varios hîc flumina circum
Fundit humus flores: hîc candida populus antro
Imminet, et lentæ texunt umbracula vites."

Being, however, very hilly, the ifland is fubject to that frequent rain which is one of the moft unpleafant circumftances attending mountainous countries. The vapours are attracted by the long range of lofty hills which ftretch from Eaft to Weft the whole length of the ifland, and in the colder months, involve the parts beneath them in almoft perpetual gloom and moifture. Yet this circumftance does not appear to affect the general health of the inhabitants refiding in the immediate neighbourhood of thefe elevations; notwithftanding the vapours thus accumulated teem with putrefcent qualities,

qualities, which I am informed, are sometimes so powerful as to taint, in a very few hours, any kind of meat in the houses immediately under the hills. This fact is most frequently experienced in the vicinity of St. Boniface and Steephill.

The *soil* of the island differs extremely in different parts; but generally speaking, is a strong and loamy earth, admirably adapted to the purposes of agriculture. It often exhibits a remarkable variety in a small district of ground; as in the parish of Brading, (towards the Eastern extremity), where the following diversities appear; in the South part, a free kind-working earth, mixed with a small proportion of sand; in the West, a light loam mixed with chalk; and in the North and East parts, a stiff clay, scarcely yielding to the operations of husbandry. The fertility of the island is almost proverbial; it having, long since, been said to produce more in one year, than its inhabitants could consume in eight. An improved husbandry has increased this fertility; and from what I have

have been able to collect, we may fairly estimate its annual produce to be at least twelve times as much as its yearly consumption.

Timber was formerly extremely plentiful in the island, but the inhabitants have had so good a market for it, at Portsmouth Dock, and the other different yards in its neighbourhood, that few extensive woods are now to be seen.* Improvident of the future, they have omitted to plant, in proportion to their cutting down; and consequently, there being no young trees to supply the place of the old ones, in a few years the Isle of Wight will be entirely robbed of its timber, and a great part of its present beauty also. The powerful reason, which perhaps has prevented the proprietors of land in this spot (and, indeed, operates with most individuals throughout the kingdom) from encouraging the growth of oak on their estates, is, the more profitable, and quick returns made to them by keeping land in an arable state. To bring this noble tree to maturity, no less than one hun-

* Of what remains, the oak and elm flourish most.

dred years are required; and it can hardly be expected, that the man of small property should forego the intermediate profits arising from his land, in an uncertain expectation of advantage to his family, at a distance of time to which he can scarcely extend his ideas of interest. Besides, it is well known that the oak requires the strongest, finest, and deepest soil for its culture; which being the most lucrative for husbandry, it is not extraordinary, that individuals not burthened with affluence, should apply it to other purposes than raising timber. These reasons, however, for neglecting the plantation of oak, though applying forcibly enough to the farmer, or landlord of small property, certainly lose great part of their effect with respect to possessors of extensive estates. To them, the inconvenience of appropriating a few acres to the purpose of planting timber, would scarcely be felt; the expences attending it would not be regarded; the loss of the intermediate profits arising from the land, would be trifling; and as large estates are frequently
entailed,

entailed, or continued in the fame family for a long feries of years, the planter of the *prefent century*, might reafonably build upon the profpect of his defcendent enjoying the fruits of his labors in the *next*.

For government to interfere at all with the management or ufe of private property, by *enforcing* in any way the planting of oak, (a practice adopted by parliament in the fixteenth century) would now be juftly deemed a trefpafs on one of the moft facred rights of the fubject; but what it cannot *compel*, it might perhaps *allure* to, by holding out honors, pecuniary rewards, or other ftimuli, to incite and encourage the proprietors of land to cultivate this valuable tree, and thereby to provide for the future navies of our country.

What timber remains, is chiefly found in the central, and Eaftern parts of the ifland. The noble woods of Sir John Barrington, Bart. at Swainfton, whofe houfe is embofomed in them, are of great extent, and contain many magnificent and valuable trees. Thofe of Wootton and

Quarr

Quarr prefent a fine fylvan fcene to the eye, covering a fuperficies of eleven hundred acres. In the parifh of Whippingham, alfo, on the Eaftern fide of the river Medina, fome valuable timber may be feen.

The principal *rivers* of the ifland are, the *Medina*, the *Yar*, and *Wootton* river. The fpreading mouth of the firft forms an ample and fecure harbour; and its ftream, after it contracts, and winds into the heart of the ifland, rolls its waters through fome very agreeable quiet fcenery, prefenting a pleafing contraft to the buftle and confufion of the port.

Wootton river, alfo, when the tide is high, is rendered extremely beautiful by the noble woods which defcend quite to the water's edge, and caft their fhades athwart it.

In the *Yar* there is nothing ftriking or picturefque.

The *springs* are in general pure and cryftalline; particularly thofe that have been filtered through the vaft ftrata of chalk, with which the

ifland

island abounds.* They are plentiful in most parts, and on the Southern coast form a pleasing accompaniment to the wild scenery of the place, by pouring forth their treasures in innumerable little cascades, pellucid as crystal, which fall from rock to rock, and gratify the ear by their murmurs, and the eye by their sparkling brilliancy.

The *inhabitants* of the island are not distinguished by any local characteristics from their countrymen on the main land; but are a vigorous, healthy, and active race. They fall naturally into the three general divisions of, gentry, yeomanry, and laboring poor.

The first class blend simplicity with refinement, and are at once hospitable and urbane. They live together in a friendly reciprocation of good offices; and strengthen their harmony by

---

* The water which has undergone this natural percolation, is so perfectly free from impurity, that it has frequently been carried to the tropics, and brought back entirely sweet.

frequent

frequent focial meetings, and the pleafures of the chace.

The yeomanry form a very refpectable clafs of people; renting, in general, eftates from one hundred pounds to four hundred, per annum. They are excellent farmers, and bear the character of kind, benevolent mafters.

The feeling and reflecting mind cannot but receive particular pleafure in contemplating the condition of the third divifion of inhabitants, the laboring poor; a defcription of people who, in other parts, are too often involved in want and wretchednefs. Among the laborers of the ifland, a general appearance of content and decency does away the ideas of poverty and mifery. They all feem comfortable and happy. Their dwellings are neat, fnug, and cleanly; to each of which is attached a little garden, kept in nice order, and planted with potatoes. Their manners are civil, inoffenfive, and incorrupted by thofe vices which are generally found amongft the lower ranks of people in the neighbourhood of great towns.

The

The above character attaches to the laborers *in general*, throughout the ifland, but applies perhaps more particularly to thofe of the rocky and mountainous regions of the South, who are chained, as it were, to their native hills, and have not been vitiated by foreign communication. It is about Steephill, Undercliff, and their neighbourhood that the poet's defcription affumes reality.

" Tho' poor the peafant's hut, his feafts tho' fmall,
He fees his little lot the lot of all;
Sees no contiguous palace rear its head,
To fhame the meannefs of his humble fhed;
No coftly lord the fumptuous banquet deal,
To make him loathe his vegetable meal;
But calm and bred in ignorance and toil,
Each wifh contracting, fits him to the foil.
Chearful at morn he wakes from fhort repofe,
Breafts the keen air and carols as he goes;
With patient angle trolis the finny deep,
Or drives his vent'rous plough-fhare to the fteep."

" At night returning, every labour fped,
He fits him down the monarch of a fhed;
Smiles by his chearful fire, and round furveys
His children's looks, that brighten at the blaze;
While his lov'd partner, boaftful of her hoard,
Difplays the cleanly platter on the board."

A a   It

'It is, however, much to be lamented, that no pains seem to have been taken, in imparting *useful knowledge* to this honeſt, and induſtrious claſs of people. When we look into other parts of the kingdom, and ſee the ſucceſs that has attended one of the nobleſt plans of general improvement among the lower ranks of ſociety, ever ſuggeſted, the eſtabliſhment of *ſunday ſchools*, by means of which, the morals of the poor are bettered, their manners civilized, and valuable inſtruction is imparted to them; we cannot but regret, that ſimilar advantages are not held out to the laboring poor of the Iſle of Wight. Both policy and morals dictate and enforce the adoption of this excellent ſyſtem. To impart inſtruction to the ignorant, is confeſſedly the duty of the higher and better informed ranks; and I believe no one will aſſert, that fulfilling this obligation has a tendency to render thoſe inſtructed, leſs valuable members of ſociety than they were, before their emancipation from profound and ſtupid ignorance. I would not take upon me to determine what *preciſe degree* of knowledge it may be neceſſary to afford to the lower ranks

of

of people; but I think we may venture to fay, all fuch information ought to be beftowed, as can tend to imprefs their minds with a proper fenfe of their obligations to God, the community, and themfelves.

It would be unpardonable were we to take leave of the inhabitants, without noticing the moft amiable part of them; the *fair females* of the ifland. The general beauty of its women has long been one of the boafts of this part of England, and any one who poffeffes a tafte for female charms, will readily acknowledge that the boaft is neither vain nor unfounded. To what phyfical caufe it may be afcribed, is difficult to fay; but certainly the girls of the ifland, of all ranks and defcriptions, have an elegance of ftature and beauty of countenance not to be obferved (in the general, I mean), in any other particular diftrict of Southern Britain.

It is here only that we may behold conftant examples of
"The form
Shap'd by the hand of harmony; the cheek,
Where the live crimfon, thro' the native white

> Soft-shooting, o'er the face diffuses bloom,
> And every nameless grace; the parted lip,
> Like the red rose-bud moist with morning dew,
> Breathing delight; and, under flowing jet,
> Or funny ringlets, or of circling brown,
> The neck light-shaded, and the swelling breast."

The *d wns* consist of a long range of hills, stretching the whole length of the island, from the town of Brading, at the Eastern extremity, to the Needle rocks at the Western one. The whole surface of these is covered with a short, sweet herbage, which affords admirable pasture for sheep; rendering the meat delicious, and the texture of the wool extremely fine. Some of these downs swell into very bold elevations, and unfold to the astonished vision prospects, vast, various, and sublime. The highest of them appears to be (from a late measurement) St. Boniface down, which rises about eight hundred and forty feet above the level of the ocean.

A late amiable naturalist, speaking of a range of chalk downs, in the upper part of Hampshire, resembling those of the island, has the following obserobfervation: " perhaps I may be fingular in my opinion, and not fo happy as to convey to you the fame idea; but I never contemplate thefe mountains, without thinking I perceive fomething analogous to *growth*, in their gentle fwellings, and fmooth fungus-like protuberances, their fluted fides, and regular hollows and flopes, that carry at once the air of vegetative dilatation and expanfion."* The idea is novel and ingenious, and feems to be founded in truth, from certain appearances of gradual enlargement which the Ifle of Wight hills have exhibited. It is a well-known fact, that, about half a century fince, Shanklin down, which ftands in the South-Eaftern part of the ifland, was not to be difcerned, from St. Catherine's, owing to the intervention of Week down, whofe magnitude and elevation completely fcreened it from the eye. A gradual, but imperceptible expanfion, however, of Shanklin down, has at length reared it to a greater bulk, and a greater height, (by at

---

* White's Nat. Hift. Selborne, p. 163.

leaft

least one hundred feet) than that of its formerly invidious neighbour.

It seems sufficiently clear, that this difference in the appearance of the two downs must have arisen rather from the *growth* of Shanklin, than the *sinking* of Week; since the latter, and all the surrounding downs, bear the same relative proportion to each other they ever did, which could not be the case, had any change taken place in its elevation or magnitude.

These downs exhibit a number of those circular marks on the grass, which Philosophy, unable herself to account satisfactorily for the phenomenon, in compliance with vulgar superstition, is content to call by the name of *fairy rings;*

> "Where
> At fall of eve the fairy people throng,
> In various game and revelry to pass
> The summer night, as village stories tell."

These appearances are generally circular, sometimes oval, and from two to twenty feet in diameter. They may easily be discovered by the

the rankness of the grass, which forms the ring, and the number of fungi or mushrooms that cover it. Various have been the conjectures relative to the cause of this phenomenon, and none perhaps more plausible than that of Doctor Darwin, who accounts for it in the following manner:

" The numerous flashes of lightning which occur every summer, are, I believe, generally discharged on the earth, and but seldom, if ever, from one cloud to another. Moist trees are the most frequent conductors of these flashes of lightning, and I am informed by purchasers of wood, that innumerable trees are thus cracked and injured. At other times larger parts or prominences of clouds, gradually sinking as they move along, are discharged on the moister parts of grassy plains. Now this knob or corner of a cloud, in being attracted by the earth, will become nearly cylindrical, as loose wool would do when drawn out into a thread, and will strike the earth with a stream of electricity perhaps two or ten yards in diameter. Now as a stream of electricity

tricity displaces the air it passes through, it is plain no part of the grass can be burnt by it, but just the external ring of this cylinder, where the grass can have access to the air, since without air nothing can be calcined. This earth, after having been so calcined, becomes a richer soil, and either fungusses or a bluer grass for many years mark the place. That lightning displaces the air in its passage, is evinced by the loud crack that succeeds it, which is owing to the sides of the aerial vacuum clapping together when the lightning is withdrawn. That nothing will calcine without air is now well understood from the acids produced in the burning of phlogistic substances; and may be agreeably seen by suspending a paper on an iron prong, and putting it into the centre of the blaze of an iron furnace; it may be held there some seconds, and may be again withdrawn without being burnt, if it be passed quickly into the flame, and out again through the external part of it, which is in contact with the air. I know," adds the Doctor, " some circles of many yards diameter, of this kind, near

Foremark

Foremark in Derbyshire, which annually produce large white fungusses, and stronger grass; and have done so, I am informed, above thirty years." The probability of this hypothesis will perhaps be allowed, when it is recollected that these gramineous circles are generally found upon open and exposed places, and never in *immediate contact* with trees, or any other free conductors of the electrical fluid.

CHAP. II.

OF THE ANCIENT CONNECTION OF THE ISLE OF WIGHT WITH THE MAIN LAND; ITS COAST; ROCKS; CAVERNS; CHINES, &c.

It is now pretty generally imagined, that the ifland, many centuries fince, was connected with, and actually made a part of, the main land. Hiftory indeed does not reach to a period previous to the exiftence of the prefent feparating ftrait; but we have recorded accounts remaining, of the waters which formed it being fo fhallow, as to leave its bottom entirely dry at low water.*

Mr. Borlafe has indeed endeavoured to prove, that the hiftorian, on whofe accounts this

* Diodorus Siculus, p. 347.

opinion

opinion is founded, spoke of one of the Caffiterides, a cluster of islands on the coast of Cornwall; and that *Ictis* (the island mentioned by him) can by no means be supposed to be the Isle of Wight. But his arguments do not appear to me convincing, particularly when opposed to the authorities produced by Mr. Whitaker, in favor of a contrary opinion.* The Cornish antiquary perceives a great absurdity in the Britons bringing their tin from such a distant place as the Belerian shores, to the Isle of Wight; but this apparent absurdity will vanish, if we reflect, according to my suggestion in an early part of this volume, that the Greeks of Marseilles, on their succeeding the Phœnicians in this traffic, might have prevailed on the Britons to remove the staple of this article, from the ports where it was originally shipped, to those of the Isle of Wight; since a removal of this nature would save the former a tedious, long, and dangerous voyage (in those days) through the Bay of Biscay, part of the Atlantic Ocean, the

* See his Hist. Manchester, vol. II. p. 177.

Straits of Gibraltar, and the Mediterranean Sea. The land-carriage of the tin, from Normandy to Languedoc, might be performed in the space of fifteen or eighteen days, whereas the circuitous navigation just mentioned would not be accomplished, by the unskilful sailors of that period, in less than five or six weeks. The appearance also of the Northern shore of the island, and the opposite one of Hampshire, seems to confirm the idea of an ancient junction between them; as they are both low, and their respective *strata* of soil, bear a near resemblance to each other.

The Northern coast of the island has nothing particularly interesting; being in general flat, or rising gradually into moderate elevations. It now and then, however, shoots out into little points and capes, which give a pleasing variety to it. The shore consists, for the most part, of hard gravel, or sand, but in many places is disfigured with dark-colored, submarine rocks. This littoral tameness on the North side is finely contrasted by the rude magnificence and stupendous

pendous horror of the Southern coast; which presents a great deal of awful and sublime scenery. In order to give an accurate idea of its appearance, it may not be amiss for us to survey it rather minutely, and trace the various promontories, bays, and windings, which it exhibits.

The bold cretaceous cliffs which form the Southern shore of the island, and stretch, with but few interruptions, from the Eastern to the Western extremities of it, commence on the Southern side of Bimbridge peninsula, rising abruptly into a perpendicular elevation of about four hundred feet. This lofty cliff is denominated *Culver* cliff,* from the circumstance of its being the resort of a great profusion of that small species of the wild pigeon, called by ornithologists the *Columba Saxatilis*, which delights in fixing its aerial abode in the clefts of inaccessible crags and lofty rocks. Here indeed, one would suppose, it might dwell in safety; but, alas! the daring foot of plunder braves

* The Saxon name of pigeon is *Culppe*.

even

even the horrors of this beetling eminence, and its fearful ledges are often visited, in the season of incubation, by him, who,

> "To the rocks
> Dire clinging, gathers his ovarious food."

This cliff affords shelter and habitations also to a particular species of *hawk*, which we shall describe in another place.

The shore now becomes suddenly very much depressed, and retires into a deep bay, called Sand-down bay, forming nearly a semi-circle of about four miles from horn to horn. The appearance of this flat beach, and of the marsh to the Northward of it, plainly indicates that the sea formerly flowed over both of them; and probably insulated the parish of Yaverland, by connecting its waters with those of Brading harbour. Towards the Western point of this bay, the shore begins to resume its wonted magnificence, leaving however its chalky appearance, and assuming a dark, ferruginous, rusty hue, (but considerably stratified) which it preserves for some distance. It here exhibits a most tremendous

dous and remarkable fiffure in the earth, called Shanklin Chine; a rent occafioned by fome partial earthquake, or other violent natural convulfion. From the perceptible commencement of this gaping chafm, to its termination on the fhore, following the various windings of the aperture, is about eight hundred yards. Its form is capricious and irregular, fomewhat refembling the leffer Greek figma; gradually increafing in depth and width, till it opens upon the fea, in a yawning of fixty yards over, and eighty-feven deep.

The rude promontory of Dunnofe now prefents itfelf, the waters of which are fo deep, that firft-rate men of war may approach within half a mile of its cliffs. The fcenery of the fhore here becomes truly wonderful. From Luccomb to Bonchurch the downs of St. Boniface heave themfelves into the clouds on the right, while huge maffes of disjointed rock, of all fhapes, and in all directions, lie fcattered in ruinous diforder below; and imprefs the mind with an idea of

thofe

those tempestuous conflicts, and elemental convulsions, which shake the very foundations of nature: when

> "The gloomy woods
> Start at the flash, and from their deep recess
> Wide flaming out, their trembling inmates shake.
> Amid Carnarvon's mountains, rages loud
> The repercussive roar; with mighty crush
> Into the flashing deep, from the rude rocks
> Of Penmanmaur heap'd hideous to the sky,
> Tumble the smitten cliffs; and Snowden's peak
> Dissolving, instant yields his wintry load.
> Far seen the heights of heathy Cheviot blaze,
> And Thule bellows through her utmost isles."

From Steephill quite to Chale, a distance of five or six miles (called not improperly Undercliff or Underway); the coast preserves an appearance, equally new, striking, and magnificent. The downs now lose their regular sloping sides gently uniting with the less animated flats below them, and terminate abruptly in a steep precipice of calcareous rock, not unlike those continuous cliffs which are seen on the banks of the Wye, in the neighbourhood of Persfield. This perpendicular precipice, which almost in a

right

right line for nearly five miles, has the appearance, if we may be allowed,

"Parva componere magnis,"

of an immense stone wall; particularly when viewed from any distance. Its height varies but little, the general elevation being about thirty or forty yards. The tract of country immediately beneath this precipitous descent, which unites with the shore, is of different breadth; from a quarter of a mile, to a mile and quarter over. It is thrown into such whimsical swellings and indentations, and lies in such romantic confusion, preserving at the same time a resemblance of parts constituting an uncouth and extraordinary whole, that I cannot help thinking it may be considered as a prodigious *land slip*, occasioned, in distant ages, by the absorption of the foundations of this vast tract into some huge cavern or gulf below, after being sapped and undermined by subterraneous waters; an opinion which is justified by various instances of similar lapses, in other parts of the kingdom, and perhaps confirmed by the rectilinear formality of the naked, remaining cliff.

From the flatnefs of this lengthened, natural wall, a very pleafing effect is found to be produced in many parts of Underway; I mean that of an *echo*, or reflection of founds, delivered loudly and diftinctly. Four fyllables have been known to be returned from thefe rocks, when uttered from their true *centrum phonicum*, which appears to be at about two hundred yards diftance. Much depends however on the *ftate of the atmofphere*, at the period of trial, fince, if it be either too rare or too denfe, it will prove unfuccefsful; for in the firft inftance the voice is attenuated and weakened, in the other it is impeded and deadened. In a ftill, clear evening, at a late hour, when the air is moderately moift, and very elaftic, the reverberation will be moft diftinct and pleafing, and would eafily deceive the young and unphilofophical.—

"Fortè puer, comitum feductus ab agmine fido,
Dixerat, Ecquis adeft? et, Adeft, refponderat Echo.
Hic ftupet; utque aciem partes divifit in omnes,
Voce, Veni, clamat magnâ. Vocat illa vocantem."

In the fingular tract of country which we have been defcribing, it is interefting to obferve how

the

the induſtrious labor of the inhabitants overcomes certain circumſtances of local inconvenience. Many ſpots of ground hereabouts lie in ſuch intricacies, among the crags of rocks and mountains, that one would imagine their ſituation ſhould ſecure them from the notice of the huſbandman. The iſlanders, however, have found means to reduce all theſe ſpots to tillage; and even thoſe which appear, from their rapid deſcent and whimſical inequalities, to be moſt incapable of being worked, yet by ploughing them ſometimes in a tranſverſe, and ſometimes in an oblique direction, they make them produce heavy and abundant crops. The operation is notwithſtanding a very laborious one; and I frequently remarked it was neceſſary for them to have five horſes to perform it. Theſe pieces of land, though thus awkwardly ſituated, are very valuable, and let for twenty ſhillings and upwards per acre.

Knowles, and the deſcent of St Catherine's ſtupendous hill, diſplay a great deal of rude, rocky ſcenery; being covered with huge fragments of cliff, tumbled and thrown about in the wildeſt confuſion. On the Weſtern ſide of the latter, another gaping fiſſure occurs, called *Blackgang* chine, a name which in ſome degree prepares one for the gloomy horrors of the chaſm. Its ſides are ſtratified with alternate layers of calcareous ſtone, and a black argillaceous earth. Through the bottom of it runs a ſtream of water, that after heavy rains is magnified into a copious torrent, which daſhes with roaring impetuoſity from one rocky fragment to another, till it reaches the mouth of the chine, down which it precipitates itſelf, in a noble perpendicular caſcade of forty feet.

The coaſt exhibits from hence a continued range of cliffs of unequal height, for the diſtance of eight or nine miles; when it forms another extenſive ſinus, called Freſhwater bay. Towards the centre of this ſweeping receſs, the ſhore again becomes flat and pebbly; and ſeems to offer but a poor bulwark againſt the thundering ſeas which ruſh in hither, when the ocean is agitated by a South-weſterly wind. Nature indeed

deed appears to have here intended a divifion of the Weftern limb of the ifland, from the other part, having brought the fpring-head of the river Yar within one hundred yards of the water's edge, and placed no obftacle to their junction in this intermediate fpace, but the low, pebbly beach above-mentioned, over which, in tempeftuous weather, the fpray of the fea eafily makes its way.

The view from the bottom of Frefhwater bay is extremely noble. On the left, the eye takes in the rugged defcent of St. Catherine's hill, the white cliffs to the Weftward of it, and three mif-fhaped, unwieldy rocks, ifolated, and detached from the land, and frowning on the waves that lafh their fides. On the right, it beholds a fhore covered with vaft fragments of broken rock, and the commencement of thofe ftupendous chalky elevations called Frefhwater cliffs; while in front, the ocean, bounded only by the horizon, clofes the fcene.

This fpot is alfo remarkable for a prodigious natural cavern, formed in the rock; to which
there

there is an approach when the tide is at ebb. It penetrates into the cliff about forty yards; gradually finking in height, and contracting in breadth, from the mouth to the bottom. Its largeſt aperture (for it has three) is a noble rude arch, ſpreading about twelve yards from ſide to ſide, and meaſuring five and twenty feet in height. The vaſt excavation we are now conſidering, like moſt other ſimilar appearances in the natural world, has probably been produced by water, which is a wonderfully active agent in the ſecret receſſes of the earth. This element, according to Doctor Goldſmith, finding ſubterraneous paſſages, and, by long degrees, hollowing the beds through which it flows, the ground above it, in time, naturally ſlips down cloſer to its ſurface, leaving the upper layers of earth or ſtone ſtill ſuſpended; the ground or rock, that ſinks upon the face of the water, forming thus the floor of the cavern, the ground or rock that keeps ſuſpended, forming the roof.

At this part the ſhore riſes into one immenſe chalk cliff, from four to ſix hundred feet in height,

height, and runs in a South-westerly direction about four miles, sometimes presenting a perpendicular elevation, at other times beetling fearfully over its excavated base. If the eye be cast down this abrupt descent, particularly during the season of incubation, it is astonished and delighted with a new and unexpected scene. Myriads of birds of various sorts and different sizes are seen, either seated on the clefts and shelvings of the rocks, or sporting in circular flights through the midway air; or floating lightly on the billows, in pursuit of their fishy prey. Meanwhile the whole sky resounds with the *rude harmony* of these winged nations; and rocks, air, and ocean present one scene of noise, bustle, and animation.*

The greater part of these *feathered clouds* are aquatic fowl, which migrate hither from the
colder

---

* Mr. Pennant has the following amusing observation, the truth of which may be fully exemplified by a visit to Freshwater cliffs. " The notes of all the sea birds are extremely harsh or inharmonious: we have often rested under the rocks attentive to the various sounds above
our

colder regions of the North, to depofit their eggs, and rear their young; of the moſt remarkable ſpecies we ſhall give an account in their proper place, but their great variety utterly precludes a particular defcription of all; for,

> " Who can recount what tranſmigrations here
> Are annual made? what nations come and go?
> And how the living clouds on clouds ariſe!
> Infinite wings! till all the plume-dark air
> And rude refounding ſhore, are one wild cry!"

The moſt ſublime part, however, of this wonderful coaſt, is the Weſtern termination of the iſland; a perpendicular chalk rock, ſcooped by the hand of Nature into an immenſe ſemi-

our heads, which, mixed with the ſolemn roar of the waves ſwelling into and retiring from the vaſt caverns beneath, have produced a fine effect. The ſharp voice of the ſea gulls, the frequent chatter of the guillemots, the loud note of the auks, the ſcream of the herons, together with the hoarſe, deep, periodical croak of the corvorants, which ſerves as a baſs to the reſt; has often furniſhed us with a concert, which, joined with the wild ſcenery that ſurrounded us, afforded in a high degree, that ſpecies of pleaſure which ariſes from the novelty, and, we may ſay, gloomy grandeur of the entertainment."—Britiſh Zoology, vol. II. p. 434.

circular

View of the Needle Rocks in the Year 1760.

circular hollow, and rearing itself six hundred feet above the pebbly shore. It is called St. Christopher's cliff. Its Northern limb is lengthened into a chain of rocks, named the *Needles*, from a lofty pointed one which formerly stood a little to the North of the remaining rocks; but (being undermined by the sea,) fell into the ocean about twenty-five years since.*

The grandeur of this scene, compared with which the mightiest works of human labor are trifling and contemptible, cannot be expressed by verbal description. To be conceived, it must be beheld; and sorry should I be for that man who, on beholding it, was not involuntarily led to a contemplation of its divine and almighty Architect; who did not feel the pious rapture of the Poet, and exclaim,

" These are thy glorious works, Parent of Good,
Almighty ! thine this universal frame
Thus wond'rous fair ; thyself how wond'rous then !

---

* The annexed plate gives a view of this singular rock, vulgarly called Lot's Wife, from its fancied resemblance to the pillar of salt, into which her improper curiosity occasioned her to be converted.

Unspeakable ; who fitt'st above these heav'ns
To us invisible, or dimly seen
In these thy lowest works."

The chalky cliffs continue round this vast promontory, the distance of somewhat more than a mile into Alum bay, when the scene is suddenly changed; they at once lose their white and precipitous appearance, and are converted into a gradual slope, consisting of various ochres, and sands of different colors, beautifully stratified in a very oblique direction. And here all grandeur ceases; the hills sink gently to the shore, and nothing now occurs but flat beach or verdant declivities.

CHAP.

CHAP. III.

THE ZOOLOGY OF THE ISLE OF WIGHT; ITS ANIMALS, REPTILES, AND FISH.

"But afk now the beafts, and they fhall teach thee; and the fowls of the air, and they fhall tell thee:"
"Or fpeak to the earth, and it fhall teach thee; and the fifhes of the fea fhall declare unto thee."
"Who knoweth not in all thefe, that the hand of the Lord hath wrought this?"

WE have hitherto confidered the magnificent exhibitions of nature in the Ifle of Wight: we fhall now defcend to her more minute but not lefs interefting operations. In the contemplation of caverns, rocks, and mountains, the mind is rather awed into aftonifhment than foftened into delight: we there behold the agency of a Being of infinite power and majefty, at whofe prefence the " earth fhakes, the heavens drop,

drop, and the waters are afraid;" but in surveying the economy of the animal and vegetable kingdoms; the exquisite mechanism with which their individuals are formed; the unerring instincts with which they are endued; and the nice adaptation of their several parts to answer the purposes for which they were created; we acknowledge the finger of a God, wise and benevolent, as he is great and powerful; who is " good to all the creatures of his hand; and whose tender mercies are over all his works."

The *fauna Vectensis* does not add much to the zoology of Hampshire. It is indeed marked by some singular *omissions* in the chain of *quadrupeds* common in every other part of England. The *fox*, who has for ages been the terror of the farmer, and the delight of the sportsman throughout Britain, was never yet found in the Isle of Wight. The harmless *badger* also, and the fetid *fitchet*, or *polecat*, are strangers to this district; which, from the absence of these animals, and its insular situation, appears to be the best calculated for the production of game of any place in in Great-Britain. And indeed it has always been famous for its hares, pheasants, and partridges.

The hare of the Isle of Wight furnishes good and constant sport to the hunter during the season. It is, I think, rather smaller than its brethren on the continent, but swift and strong. The inequalities of the island make this spot an excellent residence for the animal, and give it considerable advantages over its pursuers. The long muscular hind legs which it has, are well calculated to mount the steep downs of the island with uncommon fleetness; and it not unfrequently escapes, by distancing both hunters and dogs, at these rapid ascents.

As the hare is an animal of surprizing fecundity,* and secured from the attacks of the fox,

* They breed frequently in the year, bringing forth from two to four young ones at a litter. This wise provision of nature, in making the most innocuous and esculent animals the most fruitful, was not unnoticed by the ancient naturalists. "Benigna circa hoc natura, innocua et esculenta animalia fœcunda generavit,"—Pliny, lib. VIII. cap. lv.

and

and polecat, by the abfence of thefe deftructive vermin in this part, we may naturally fuppofe they would be found in very great plenty throughout the ifland. And indeed this was the cafe till within thefe thirty or forty years; but as a *Roman tafte** for thefe animals has arifen amongft us, and they are confidered as *tit-bits* by modern epicurifm, the midnight poacher finds it well worth while to employ all his fkill, and run every rifk, in the capture of the hare; a practice which of courfe muft thin the breed extremely. There remain, however, fufficient for the fport of the gentlemen of the ifland.

There are few difagreeable reptiles in the ifland. Such as occur, are found in the lower, fandy parts of it; the other fpots being freed from them by the elevation and expofure of their fituation. Many *vipers* indeed are met with in

---

* The Romans were very partial to this animal:
"Inter quadrupedes gloria prima lepus."——Martial.
And its fhoulder was reckoned a moft delicate morfel;
"Fœcundi leporis fapiens fectabitur *armos*."——Horace.
See my "Antiquitates Culinariæ." Quarto, Blamire, 1791.

the chalky and stony places, and the largest I ever saw, I had nearly trodden upon, in the parish of Wootton, in the outskirts of Coombly wood, in August, 1792. Had my foot, however, come in contact with this animal, no injury could have ensued to me from the pressure, as it was utterly incapable of revenging the insult. This incapacity had been produced by its voraciousness, as was evident on an examination of the reptile. We then found that it had attempted to gorge a frog, (at least three times as large in circumference as the thickest part of its own body,) but being unable to accomplish the task entirely, one of the legs and thighs of its prey continued to depend from the viper's mouth, and effectually prevented it from closing the jaws and excluding its poison. The animal indeed (as is the case with all the serpent kind after satisfying their voracity,) was in a state of torpor, which rendered it apparently insensible of our approach or observation, and unable to express any tokens of indignation when we destroyed it. On measuring it when dead, it was found to be exactly twenty-nine inches long.

On

On contemplating this animal, one of the moſt remarkable circumſtances relating to it, appears to be the faculty it thus poſſeſſes, of extending its jaws, throat, and ſtomach ſo conſiderably, as to render them capable of admitting a ſubſtance much thicker than any part of its body. In the ſingular conformation of its parts, to accompliſh this purpoſe, the wiſdom of providence ſtrikingly manifeſts itſelf. The head of the viper is broad and flat, having a wide mouth of very uncommon and diſproportionate magnitude. This permits the jaws to gape to a great extent; but the aperture would ſtill be inſufficient for the admiſſion of the animal's prey, were not the capability of its diſtention increaſed by the following nice contrivance. The jaws are not united together at the bottom, as in the human mouth, by a proceſs reſembling a pair of hinges; but connected by a ſtrong muſcle, the elaſticity of which is ſuch, as to keep the features firm when not in action, and to allow their being ſtretched to an immoderate extent, when the ſize or form of the animal's food requires it. The gullet or throat receives the aliment from the

mouth,

mouth, and being very capacious and elaftic, eafily accommodates itfelf to the magnitude and figure of it. From hence a part only immediately finds its way into the ftomach, a receptacle by no means fo large as the gullet; here it continues till it be reduced by the action of digeftion into chyle, which going off in the natural way, affords room for the remaining parts to be abforbed by the ftomach, and digefted.

Thefe reptiles are viviparous, but fortunately for mankind not very prolific.* The poifon of their bite is fully eftablifhed; and the effects of it, if there be no fpeedy application to the wound, extremely frightful, and many times fatal. The fimpleft and moft ready cure, in cafe of an injury from a viper, is a brifk fomentation of the wounded limb with warmed fallad oil; and taking about a jill of the fame liquid internally.

* That is, as Ariftotle expreffes it, "Εν αυτοις μεν ωοτοκει το τελειον ωον, εξω δε ζωοτοκει."—De Gen. Animal. lib. III. cap. ii. " *Within* them they bear a perfect egg, (wherein the young one is contained) but they *bring forth* their young alive." They produce from fix to ten at a time; copulate in May, and are about three months in geftation.

The only insect of any curiosity, which my occasional walks through the island have given me an opportunity of discovering, is the *gryllus talpa*, or mole-cricket. The character and manners of this little creature, which is perfectly inoffensive, are well deserving notice, particularly as its homely, and indeed hideous figure, are apt to excite emotions of dread and abhorrence, neither of which need be entertained against it. The only one I have seen in this part of Hampshire occurred in a wet meadow in the heart of the island. It had been dug up by a lad who was grouting for earth-worms; and had filled him with astonishment and apprehension. The spade was just lifted for dividing the harmless insect in twain, when my presence and intreaty prevented the meditated blow. On examining this insect, it appeared to be of a very dark brown color, and little more than two inches in length. Its body was scaly; furnished with two long, pointed wings, and as many hairy tails. The most remarkable parts about it, however, were the fore-feet, which have some resemblance to a human hand, and are admirably formed for making those subterraneous excavations wherein the animal resides, and deposits its eggs. Strong, webbed, and a little incurvated, the mole-cricket works with its paws at a prodigious rate, and will burrow its way through a whole ridge of leguminous plants, (of the roots of which it is very fond) in the course of a single night. With these instruments, also, its neat habitation (which is a room about the size of an hen's egg) is quickly formed, and guarded with various winding passages, and curious approaches to it. This domicilium is generally, in the summer time, placed within six inches of the surface of the ground, and herein the female lays her eggs, from one hundred to one hundred and fifty; but towards winter, instinct, ever faithful to its office, informs the little being that in order to secure his tender offspring he must get deeper into the soil, and retire from the influence of the frost. Again therefore he sets to work, and in a short time completes with his little webbed feet, a commodious hybernaculum, about fourteen inches below the surface of the ground. Hither he retires with his family, and patiently waits for the return of genial suns, and warmer seasons, when he again takes possession of his summer abode.

The chief food of the mole-cricket consists of roots and vegetables, for which he sometimes travels at night, by the assistance of his wings, to a considerable distance. Before morning he generally returns to his subterraneous habitation, and, wonderful to tell! is found (by the minute investigations of naturalists and anatomists,) to be employed there during the day chiefly in *ruminating*, or chewing the cud.

What purposes these little, but curious insects may answer in the scale of creation, we cannot at present apprehend, and shall perhaps ever remain ignorant of them. That, however, they fulfil certain ends, and those beneficial ones, cannot be doubted; as they are the creatures of an Artist who made nothing in vain, and who formed every *part* to assist and co-operate towards the good of the *whole*. Viewed in this light, even the mole-cricket becomes a source

of

of edification; since it may at least serve to humble the pride of *human knowledge*, by exemplifying the truth of the Philosopher's observation; *Ea quæ scimus sunt pars minima eorum quæ ignoramus.*

The *fish* found on the coast of the island are chiefly such as frequent the Southern shores of Britain. Now and then, indeed, these innoxious tribes are disturbed by the *shark*, who is either brought from the Baltic, or the tropics. In these cases he comes,

"Lur'd by the scent
Of steaming crouds, of rank disease, and death."

following vessels, the crews of which are unhealthy, and afford him luxurious meals by their occasional dissolution. Sharks have been shot in the strait that separates the island from the opposite shore, and been seen even within the harbour of Cowes. They make, however, but a short stay in this neighbourhood; and either return to the regions from whence they came, or go more to the Westward, in search of the droves of pilchards on the Cornish coast.

The *porpesse* also is perpetually seen on the coasts of the island, " tempesting the deep" with its unwieldy gambols. It is a very disgusting fish to the eye, being almost black in color, with a head like a hog, and from three to six feet in length.

During the whiting and herring season, it is very amusing to watch these animals in pursuit of their food, which is composed of the smaller fish; and to remark the various arts by which they accomplish the great end of satisfying their voracity. An excellent naturalist[*] compares their exertions, at this time, to those of a pack of hounds after a fox; and indeed there is a great resemblance in the operations of both. Their eagerness also, when thus engaged, equals that of the dog, and frequently renders the porpesse so blind to its safety, that he will dash headlong upon shoals from which he never can recede; rather than give up the pursuit. It is either by an accident of this nature, or by an injury or indisposition which prevents him keeping the seas,

[*] Pennant, Brit. Zoology, vol. III.

that the porpesse is now and then forced on our shores, and found either dead or expiring. When this happens, the carcase proves to be no contemptible treasure to the finder; for the quantity of fat with which the flesh is surrounded, being well boiled, is converted into a very excellent and valuable oil. The lean also of this fish is in some parts of the world used for the table; but proves, to a palate not habituated to it, a very rank and disagreeable viand.

The mutations of fashions and tastes, however, in the line of eating, have been not a little whimsical, even in our own country; since the porpesse, which we now turn from with loathing and abhorrence, was eaten with avidity by the old English epicure. Ancient cookery exhausted all its art in mixing sauces for this delectable morceau; and there was no entertainment of any magnificence till the sixteenth century, at which the porpesse, either bodily or in junks, did not find a respectable place.*

* Vide my "Antiquitatates Culinariæ, or Curious Tracts relating to old English Cookery." Quarto; Blamire, 1791.

There is another fish of a curious form and singular history, which is often fished up by the dredgers on the island shores. This is the *loligo*, or great cuttle-fish, whose bones are the well known white, oval substances, found on the beach in many parts of the island. This aquatic animal, which the naturalists place in the *vermes* class, exibits a very hideous and deformed appearance. It is from eighteen inches to two feet in length, and covered with a thin dark colored skin. To the eye it seems to be of the consistence of jelly; strengthened, consolidated, and defended as it were by a bone on the upper part of the back. For the convenience of feeding itself, it possesses eight arms, placed with great regularity round its mouth, each of which is thickly set with a multitude of small concave dises, that enable it to adhere, with inconceivable tenacity, to rocks or stones when it chuses to be quiescent. Exclusive of these arms it has two *tentacula*, or feelers, of considerable length, which it is able to extend or contract at pleasure. With these it seizes upon the small fry that

com-

compose its food, which having entangled, they immediately commit the prey to the management of the eight arms, while themselves are again extended in search of further plunder. The eyes are seated immediately beneath the *tentacula*; and a little below them is discovered a curious mouth, which in shape and substance nearly resembles the beak of a parrot.

As this fish is formed without any external weapons of defence, and by no means made for contest or exertion, it would fare but ill amid the dangers of the deep, and the numerous enemies that surround it, had not providence wisely afforded it a means of safety, which enables it to escape mischance, and continue the propagation of its kind. This arises from a secretion of a black fluid, nearly resembling the best ink, contained in a bladder under the belly of the fish. No sooner does the animal perceive himself to be in danger, from the pursuit of an enemy which he can neither outswim nor contend with, than he emits (by the anus) a certain portion of his dingy liquor; this immediately discolors the circumambient waters, and precludes the purſuer from ſeeing his deſtined prey, which, wrapped in impenetrable darkneſs, quietly ſinks to the bottom, and there remains till the danger be overpaſt.

Theſe remarkable means of ſelf-preſervation, did not elude the obſervation of the ancient naturaliſts, who all make mention of them; and particularly Oppian, in the following pretty manner:

"Th'endanger'd cuttle thus evades his fears,
And native hoards of fluid ſafety bears.
A pitchy ink peculiar glands ſupply,
Whoſe ſhades the ſharpeſt beams of light defy:
Purſu'd he bids the ſable fountains flow,
And wrapt in clouds eludes th'impending foe.
The fiſh retreats unſeen, while ſelf-born night,
With pious ſhade befriends her parent's flight."*

The *launce, ammodytes,* or *ſand-eel,* is a delicate little fiſh, found on the ſandy ſhores of the iſland. It being both a good bait for other ſpecies, and excellent eating in itſelf, the fiſhermen take ſome trouble in procuring them. At

* Jones's Oppian's Halieut. lib. III.

the recefs of the tide, they are to be found about fourteen inches below the furface, and are eafily turned up by a light fpade, or tridented fork. The iflanders call them the *fand-fprat*, from the place of their refidence; into which they bore with great dexterity and difpatch.

Here alfo is found the *filiqua*, a fpecies of the *folen*, or razor; fo called from the exact refemblance of its fhell to the haft of that inftrument. I believe the iflanders are unacquainted with the excellence of this fifh; fince I did not find they ever made a practice of taking them, although it is evident they are fufficiently plentiful, on the fandy parts of the coaft, from the numbers of caft fhells which occur, and the holes of their habitations vifible at low water.

The flender form of this fhell enables its inhabitant to fink it eafily into the fand, which it does in a perpendicular direction, to the depth of nearly two feet. When the fifh requires food, it afcends from this dark retreat, and difcovers one end of the fhell a few inches above the furface of the fand; from this the body is feen to be be protruded, and actively employed in the search of such minute insects as constitute its prey.

The *siliqua* is only to be caught at the recess of the tide; and so vigilant is it in providing for its own safety, that it requires great circumspection to surprize it even then. In this case, the fisherman takes some salt, and places a small quantity of it round the perforation in the sand wherein the fish resides. This quickly melting penetrates to the *siliqua*, who is led from thence to believe the tide is risen, and accordingly elevates himself to the surface to seek for food. A moment, however, convinces it of the deceit, and if the fisherman be not extremely active, his destined prey escapes him, by sinking instantaneously into its dark and deep retreat, from whence it is not a second time to be allured.

The *mytilus edulis*, or eatable muscle, is found in many parts of the island shores, but appears not to be regarded much, from the opinion of its possessing some noxious, nay poisonous qualities. The idea, however, is slanderous and
without

without foundation, as the fish itself is a wholesome and nutritious food. What occasions the disagreeable effects sometimes experienced after eating muscles, is swallowing inadvertently the little mass of hair or silky web, found in the middle of the fish, with which it attaches itself when alive to rocks and stones. This is very pernicious and highly indigestible, producing that sickness, swelling, &c. which raw silk, cobwebs, or any thing of the same nature, is found, if swallowed, to occasion.*

On opening the muscle, there is generally discovered a small crab, called the *pisum*, or peacrab, who seems to be the voluntary inhabitant of this bivalve. The ancients fancifully imagined, that this minute insect was purposely placed in

---

* The singular conformation of the organs of this marine animal is said to be this: It has a mouth furnished with two fleshy lips; its intestine begins at the bottom of the mouth, passes through the brain, and makes a number of circumvolutions through the liver; on leaving this organ it goes on straight into the heart, which it penetrates, and ends in the anus; near which the lungs are placed, and through which it breathes!—Goldsmith's Animated Nature, vol, VII. p. 42.

the

the shell of the muscle, and other fish of the same class, to assist, by its sagacity, the stupidity of its host, in acquiring food and avoiding danger. When the friendly pair feel inclined to eat, the muscle opens its shells, and permits the little lodger to travel forth in quest of provender. As soon as he has procured a supply, he returns to the sluggish muscle, enters the shell, and divides the plunder with him. But should he, on going out, perceive any of the *polypus* race, (the sworn enemies of the mytilus tribe,) in the neighbourhood, he instantly hurries to his testaceous home, communicates the alarm, and all danger is immediately prevented by the muscle firmly closing his impenetrable shells.*

All the submarine rocks and stones on the coast of the island afford protection to the *patella vulgata*, or common limpet; and to these this fish attaches itself with the most obstinate adhesion. The difficulty of separation indeed is such, that the fishermen are deterred from attempting to collect limpets for sale; though

* Pliny. Antiquitates Culin. in preliminary discourse.

such

such as have patience sufficient to disengage them from the places to which they are affixed, are rewarded for their trouble by an extremely good and nourishing viand.

Various species of turbinated shells, chiefly of the *buccinum* or *welk* kind, are picked up on these shores. As the natural inhabitants of these affect the deep recesses of the ocean, the shells are never found with their original possessors alive. It frequently happens, however, that on taking them up they appear to be tenanted by a kind of *crab;* the claws and legs of which discover themselves at the mouth or opening of the shell. This lodger is called the *bernard*, or *hermit-crab*, and curiously exhibits the wonderful operations of animal instinct. As the hinder parts of the hermit's body are tender and naked, unprotected by that shelly covering which its crustaceous brethren possess, perpetual injuries would happen to it, had not nature provided it with a foresight which serves to guard it from external accident. Taught by this, the hermit-crab seeks for the roomy cavity of some forsaken

welk;

welk, into which it wriggles itself, and there continues till its increased size obliges it to look out for an habitation of greater dimensions. It then leaves its temporary protector, and traverses the coast with patient affiduity, in search of another abode, to which when found it attaches itself, as to the former one, by means of a strong hook placed at the extremity of its tail. So kindly has providence bestowed even on the most minute and contemptible animals, the means of comfort and self-preservation!

The Southern shore of the island abounds with crustaceous fish of all sorts. The *lobster* and *crab* in particular are found in great plenty, and of uncommon size and excellence. Of the former, I have seen an individual that weighed six pounds and an half; and I am informed the latter will arrive to an equal magnitude. The plentiful production of this fish on a particular part of the shore, at the back of the island, has occasioned a neighbouring village to be called Crab-Niton.

CHAP.

CHAP. IV.

OF THE ORNITHOLOGY OF THE ISLE OF WIGHT.

"Quæ multæ glomerantur aves!"

THOUGH Nature have been rather thrifty in her diftribution of *quadrupeds* to the Ifle of Wight; yet fhe makes ample amends by the number and variety of the *feathered tribes*, which are either conftant refidents in this part of England, or flock hither during the feafon of incubation. At this period the lofty chalk cliffs are all one living fcene, and exhibit a fingular appearance of univerfal buftle.

Amongft the winged emigrants who thus vifit the fhores of the ifland, to fulfil the great command of nature, and rear their tender young,

Gg there

there are some which are seen only occasionally on these rocks; and who appear to be brought hither by accident or caprice, rather than the force of instinct. Thus for instance, the *eagle* has been known to incubate among the crags of Culver cliff. The beetling brows of this eminence appear to offer an eligible habitation for this predacious bird, which, according to Job's sublime description of it, is partial to these elevated situations:

" Doth the eagle mount up at thy command, and make her nest on high?"

" She dwelleth and abideth on the rock, upon the crag of the rock, and the strong place."

" From thence she seeketh the prey, and her eyes behold afar off."

" Her young ones also suck up blood; and where the slain are, there is she."*

The last eagle known to build in Culver cliff (according to the information I could obtain,) came there in the year 1780. An adven-

---

* Job, chap. xxxix. ver. 27, 28, 29, 30. Pliny, speaking of the same birds, says; " Nidificant in petris et arboribus."—Lib. X. sect. iv.

turous

turous countryman, who had frequently defcended the rock for the eggs of its other winged tenants, having watched the eagle from the neft, paid a vifit to it alfo. He found this fabrication to be of confiderable fize, and formed of fticks and rufhes laid alternately; containing one folitary young bird. This he took, but not knowing how to manage it, the eaglet foon died.

It is probable the parent bird had come from the Northern parts of Wales, or the craggy cliffs of the Weftern Ifles; fince the offspring appeared to be of the *ringtail* fpecies, a fort very common in thofe places. It is, however, but very rarely that this noble bird builds its ayry in a fpot fo diftant from the natural place of its abode. The vigor of this race fits it for inhabiting the colder regions of the North. Here it dwells in folitary majefty, furrounded by filence and defolation; its fiercenefs and voracity giving additional horrors to the favage fcenery of its unfrequented domain;

"High from the fummit of a craggy cliff
Hung o'er the deep, fuch as amazing frowns

On utmost *Kilda's* shore, whose lonely race
Resign the setting sun to Indian worlds;
The royal eagle draws his vig'rous young,
Strong pounc'd, and ardent with paternal fire."

To an observer of the manners of birds, nothing is more amusing than to remark the various little devices which the parents will use, during the season of incubation, to draw any intruding footstep from the spot that conceals their offspring. Thus, for example, a pewit, or lapwing, the moment it is aware of any approach to her young, immediately takes flight, and wheeling in circles round the head of the enemy, endeavours to engage his attention, and by degrees to draw him from her nest. A partridge also, if she observe a dog or man coming towards her helpless covey, will hop away as if wounded, with a tumbling kind of gait, that the intruder may be induced to pursue her, rather than molest the offspring. But of all the different modes suggested by animal στοργη for the preservation of the young, that of the eagle seems to be the most efficacious; and indeed forms an

admirable

admirable *accompaniment* to the rude and fearful scenery of the precipices wherein these birds usually fabricate their lofty citadels.

As no naturalist (to the best of my recollection) has mentioned this particular in the history of the eagle, the reader will not be displeased in being made acquainted with it by the following anecdote:

A few summers since, a gentleman, making the tour of Wales, passed through the county of Carnarvon. Having furnished himself with a guide, he visited every part of this romantic coast. One day, in strolling amongst the rocks and precipices with which it abounds, he found himself suddenly separated from his companion. At that moment, a dismal hollow moan assailed his ear from below. Shortly afterwards he heard it again: and it was repeated, with slight interruptions, for two or three minutes. His imagination, prepared to receive impressions of terror from the ruggedness and desolation of the surrounding rocks, immediately painted to him the unfortunate guide fallen from the precipice,

and

and dafhed to pieces on the crags beneath. In a fhort time, however, his mind was relieved from this painful idea, by the appearance of the fuppofed fufferer, who had been hidden from his obfervation by the prominent jutting of an enormous rock. On being joined by him, he communicated the extraordinary circumftance which had occurred, and the founds of diftrefs that even then rang in his ear. But his apprehenfions were foon calmed by the guide, who informed him, they proceeded from fome eagle in the vicinity; with which bird it was cuftomary, during the feafon of incubation and before the young ones had quitted the neft, to emit the doleful founds that had alarmed him, in order to entice away any intruder from the place of its abode.

When the diverfion of falconry was a noble, and even royal amufement, Culver cliffs were in fome degree of repute, from their producing in great abundance a fmall fpecies of *hawk*, of great ftrength and fpirit, much ufed in fporting for partridges, and other birds of an equal or inferior fize.

size. As this amusement is, however, now obsolete, the breed, which still continues, is allowed to build its aerial nests, and pursue its depredations on young game, pigeons, &c. without molestation. I take it to be the *falco nisus* of Linnæus.

I have before mentioned the multitude of migrating birds, which may be seen on the rocky shores of the island, during the early summer months. Most of these come hither, merely for the purpose of depositing their eggs on the ledges of the cliffs, and rearing their young; which business being performed they return to their more northerly habitations. Of these species the most curious and remarkable are, the puffin; the razorbill; the guillemot; and the cormorant, or, as it is vulgarly called in these parts, the *Isle of Wight parson*.

The *puffin* usually resorts to this coast about the latter end of April. On its arrival, it immediately looks out for a proper place for the deposition of its egg; it seldom, or never, laying more than one: a crevice in the rock, or a hole in the ground near the fhore, beft ferves this important purpofe. Being thus provided with an habitation, the female produces her burthen, which fhe and her faithful confort continue alternately to cover and protect, till the young bird is excluded from the fhell. This happens about the middle of June, when nothing can equal the buftle and anxiety of the dams. They are now to be feen flying in circular rings about the aperture of their nefts, fhewing, as it were, the ufe of their pinions to the unpractifed young, and encouraging them, by a thoufand little arts, to commit themfelves to the vacant air, or drop into the watery wafte. This bufinefs, however, once finifhed, the στοργη ceafes. Nature has accomplifhed the important end of introducing the rifing generation properly to the world; and it would now be a wafte of affection, were the dam to continue its parental fondnefs. The moment, therefore, that inftinct informs the older birds it is time for them to depart from their fummer habitation, they obey its intimations. No paternal ties can protract their ftay; fuch of

their

their offspring as are able to accompany their flight, join the migrating hoft, whilft the more feeble young ones are left to fhift for themfelves.

I cannot give fo accurate an idea of this fingular bird, which is equally curious in perfon as in manners, as by tranfcribing the excellent defcription of it, drawn by the faithful pen of our Britifh Zoologift.

"This bird," fays he, "weighs about twelve ounces; its length is twelve inches; the breadth from tip to tip of the wings extended, twenty-one inches: the bill is fhort, broad at the bafe, compreffed on the fides, and running up to a ridge, triangular, and ending in a fharp point: the bafe of the upper mandible is ftrengthened with a white narrow prominent rim, full of very minute holes; the bill is of two colors, the part next the head of a bluifh grey, the lower part red: in the former is one tranfverfe groove or furrow, in the latter three; the fize of the bill is one inch and three quarters long; and the bafe of the upper mandible one inch broad."

"The

" The *irides* are grey, and the edges of the eye-lids of a fine crimson; on the upper eye-lid is a singular callous substance, grey, and of a triangular form; on the lower is another of an oblong form; the crown of the head, whole upper part of the body, tail, and covert feathers of the wings are black; the quill-feathers are of a dusky hue."

" The cheeks are white, and so full of feathers as to make the head appear very large, and almost round; the chin of the same color, bounded on each side by a broad bed of grey: from the corner of each eye is a small separation of the feathers, terminating at the back of the head. The neck is encircled with a broad collar of black; but the whole lower part of the body, as far as is under water, is white."

" Tail black, composed of sixteen feathers: legs small, of an orange color, and placed so far behind as to disqualify it from standing, except quite erect; resting not only on the foot, but the whole length of the leg; this makes the rise of the puffin from the ground very difficult, and

it

it meets with many falls before it gets on wing; but when that is effected, few birds fly longer or stronger."*

The *razor-bill* is found among the lofty crags of Freshwater, and St. Christopher's cliffs, about the beginning of May. Here it is that the female deposits her single egg (for they never lay but one at a time) on the bare level of some rocky ledge, that beetles over the beach below. This egg is enormously large in proportion to the size of the bird, being three inches in length; its color is either a dirty white, or a sea green, thickly set with a variety of irregular black spots.† To acquire these, and to procure the feathers of the young puffins, it is customary with many of the islanders to descend the tremendous precipices where they are found, by the assistance of a strong rope, attached to a crow bar fixed in the ground

* Brit. Zool. p. 431. Quarto.

† These are erroneously, though commonly, called puffin's eggs; whereas the egg of that bird is much smaller, and entirely white.

above. When the eggs are gotten, they may be purchafed at about nine pence a dozen; and being boiled hard, are by many people much efteemed. The yolk is then rich and well flavored, but the white very infipid, and fomewhat difagreeable to the eye, having the appearance of a dingy tranfparent jelly. If the fituation of the egg be obferved, as ordered by the parent bird, it will be found to be moft wonderfully and curioufly placed; with a balance fo nice and exact, that fhould it be once removed, it is out of the power of human art to reftore it to its former equilibrium. Indeed the danger of the egg rolling off the fmooth level on which it is depofited, from the agitation of the winds, or other external caufes, is fo inftinctively known by the female razor-bill, that when once it is brought forth, fhe feldom forfakes it till the young one is excluded; being regularly fed by the affiduous male, who is conftantly on the wing feeking provifion for his faithful partner, during this tedious incubation. In the mean time, fhould any plunderer deprive this patient creature

ture of her folitary egg, fhe immediately fupplies its place with another; and if the theft be repeated twice or thrice, fhe will as often produce a frefh one; though, wonderful to tell, fhe never thinks of laying a fecond if her firft-born be left undifturbed.

The razor-bill is a handfome bird, about eighteen inches long, and twenty-fix broad; its head, back, and wings black; its neck and belly white. The bill is two inches long; fomewhat crooked, ftrong, and fharp; having a broad tranfverfe groove of white, crofling each mandible. The legs are black, and placed very far back, which gives the bird the fame erect appearance when ftanding, as the puffin has; and nothing is more laughable, but at the fame time more curious, than to behold long ranks of thefe birds thickly planted fide by fide, on the different ledges of the rocks, in a pofture, which, though natural to them, has a moft affected and abfurd appearance.

The *guillemot* alfo migrates to the Ifle of Wight rocks, to produce and rear its offspring.

It

It generally accompanies the other aquatic birds before defcribed, both in their advent and departure. Like them too, it only lays one egg, of a pale blue, fpotted with black blotches, or marked with numerous interfecting lines. Its figure is not inelegant, though it do not boaft the brilliant colors of other birds; being, on the head, neck, back, and wings, of a deep moufe color, with the belly perfectly white. The bill is about three inches long, ftraight, and tapering to a very fharp point.

Naturalifts have given to this bird the opprobrious name of the *foolifh guillemot,* from its not changing its fituation when fhot at. But I am inclined to think, from obfervations which I have perfonally made, that this conduct of the bird is rather a beautiful example of inftinctive animal affection, than a fpecimen of ftupidity. The attachment of thefe aquatic birds to their offspring, is (whilft it continues) ardent beyond apprehenfion; and the reafon of the older birds thus neglecting to fly from danger, when it becomes too obvious to them to be miftaken, is,

their

their difinclination to remove from their young ones, which would not be able to accompany them in their flight.

Whilft thefe various fpecies of migrating birds continue in the neighbourhood of the Needle rocks, it is a common diverfion with the fportf- men of thefe parts, to form parties for the purpofe of fhooting them; a barbarous practice, and without excufe; fince the wounded carcafes of thefe unfufpecting vifitors can be applied to no one ufe after they are deftroyed. But fuch are the delights of

> " The fteady tyrant man,
> Who, with the thoughtlefs infolence of pow'r,
> Inflam'd beyond the moft infuriate wrath
> Of the worft monfter that e'er roam'd the wafte,
> For fport alone purfues the *cruel game*,
> Amid the beamings of the gentle days."

The *cormorant** is not, properly fpeaking, a bird of migration. It builds in, and inhabits the

---

* The proper name of this bird is *corvorant*, from *corvus* crow, and *vorans* devouring; an appellation it well deferves, from its incredible voracity, infatiable gluttony, and rapid digeftion.

immenfe

immenfe precipices of Frefhwater, for the better part of the year. During the winter, however, the voracious plunderer may be feen, purfuing his depredations in the rivers and creeks, for many miles around. Here this folitary favage is on the perpetual watch for prey; tortured with unquenchable hunger, occafioned by an infinite multitude of worms, which inhabit his infide, and, like the dogs of Milton's Sin, would make his bowels their repaft, did he not fupply their voracity by unceafing repletion. For this purpofe, the miferable glutton is feen continually diving after the fifh, which his piercing eye can difcern at a great depth in the water; or perched upon fome folitary elevation, enjoying a temporary refpite from labor, and the attacks of his internal enemies. During thefe moments of idlenefs and eafe, he is often found feated in a lofty tree; a fituation fomewhat fingular for a water fowl, and which indeed (according to the obfervation of Ariftotle) the cormorant alone, of all birds of that clafs, makes ufe of. It is this generally unobferved circumftance, in the hiftory

of

of the cormorant, that our great Poet has laid hold of, when he introduces Satan ufurping the figure of that bird, and perching upon a tree, to make his obfervations on our firft parents:

> "Thence up he flew, and on the tree of life,
> The middle tree, and higheft there that grew,
> Sat like a *cormorant*."*

An admirable vehicle, from its voracity and bafenefs, for the Devil to make ufe of, whilft devifing fchemes of death and deftruction.

Nature feems to have intended a check upon human gluttony, by rendering thofe quadrupeds and birds, which are moft remarkable for an intemperate indulgence of the appetite, the moft hateful and offenfive. The cormorant is a proof of this, than which bird no other is more voracious in feeding, nor at the fame time, more difagreeable in perfon, deteftable in fmell, or difgufting in manners; an inftance, amongft num-

* Paradife Loft, book IV. line 193.

berlefs others, of the *moral inftruction* which might be gleaned from every part of nature, if we would but perufe her ample volume.

The ifland has always produced abundance of game. As early as the reign of Henry VIII. we find that the pheafants and partridges of the royal demefnes here, engaged the attention of our monarchs. This prince, who was a great fportfman, and more particularly devoted to *hawking*, amufed himfelf occafionally that way in the ifland. Great depredations, however, were committed by the farmers, and lower ranks of people, on the birds, (for *poaching* was practifed even three centuries ago) which occafioned the following mandate from Henry, to Richard Worfley, Efq. who was then Captain of the Ifle of Wight. It bears date in 1541:

" Trufty and well beloved we grete you well and being crediblye enfourmed that o^r. Games of Partriche and Fefant w^{t}in that our Ifle of Wight is muche decayed by the pmiffion and fufferaunce of fuche lewd pſons as for their pryvate Lucres

contrary

contrary to our Lawes and pleafure doo dailye w:t. netts and other Engyns take the fame. You fhall underftande that myndyng to havie the fayd Games of Patriches and Fefant cherifhed w:tin our fayde Ifle as wel for our difporte and Paftyme if we fhould chaunce to repayre thither as for our Furniture at fundry our Hono:rs. Manors and Houfes which from tyme to tyme we intende to replenifhe with the fcore of the fame Ifle as nede fhall requyre Our pleafure and commaundement is that you fhall not only uppon monicon to be by you hereof given to the Inhabitaunts of the fayde Ifle have diligent regarde and vigilant Eye that no man of no degree or condition kill any Fezant or Partriche w:t. net Engyne or Hawk on any our propre lands in the fame Ifle, taking the Netts and Engyns of all fuch as fhall attempte the contrary and further punifheng the ptyes foe offending as to your Wifdom fhall be thought convenyent. But alfo that you fhall advife all the Reft of the Owners and Inhabitaunts there at o:r. con-

tem-

templacon alſo to ſpare the ſame games in their own grounds, ſpeally abſtaining to take or ſuffre to be taken any Feſant or Partriche wt. netts and ſuch Engyns as totally deſtroyeth the Brede of the ſame wherein you ſhall doo unto us acceptable ſervice. And theiſe our Lres ſhall be your ſufficient Warraunt and diſcharge in that behalf. Given undre our Signet, at or. manor of Otland the 19th. day of Decembre the 32 yere of or. Reign."*

The *woodcock* is found in the Iſle of Wight during the uſual ſeaſon of his viſits to this part of Europe. Two or three ſtragglers generally arrive before the appearance of the great flock, which always manages to reach the land after ſunſet; a well-informed friend, who is alſo a ſportſman, informed me, that one or two had been ſeen this year as early as the middle of September, but inſtances of this premature

---

* Append. to Worſley's Hiſt. Iſle of Wight, No. XXXVII.

advent are by no means common. They continue here till the latter end of March, after which time it seldom happens that they are met with. One or two pair, indeed, have been known to remain and breed, as has been the case, though rarely, in some other parts of the kingdom.

Many stories have been told of *swallows*, and other British *hirundines*, being found during the winter, in a torpid state, in holes and crevices of the island cliffs; but, after the minutest enquiry, I do not see reason to credit any of the relations. Indeed, the general migration of the *hirundo* tribes is now so fully established, that the naturalist will be disinclined to give credit to any thing less than ocular demonstration, for their continuance during the winter with us. In forward springs they have been observed here as early as the eighteenth and twentieth of February: and at the latter end of September may be seen assembled in large flocks, waiting for a fair gale, to waft them to Southern latitudes,

and

and warmer climes. Indeed they need every affiftance from wind and weather, fince we find they wing their arduous flight as far as Senegal, and other parts of Africa.*

* M. Adanfon's Voyage to Senegal, p. 121. The *Poet of Nature* has, with his ufual accuracy, painted the *manners* of thefe tribes, previous to their departure from their fummer abodes:

" When autumn fcatters his departing glooms,
Warn'd of approaching winter, gather'd play
The fwallow people, and tofs'd wide around
O'er the calm fky, in convolution fwift,
The feathered eddy floats, rejoicing once,
Ere to their winter flumbers they retire.
In clufters hung beneath the mould'ring bank,
And where, unpierc'd by frofts, the wint'ry cavern
    fweats;
Or rather into warmer climes convey'd,
With other kindred birds of feafon there,
They twitter chearful, till the vernal months
Invite them welcome back; for thronging now,
Innum'rous wings are in commotion all."—Thompfon.

CHAP.

CHAP. V.

OF THE BOTANY OF THE ISLE OF WIGHT.

It is not our intention to enter into a minute and scientific account of the various plants to be found in this extensive district; since this alone would make a copious work. The object of these pages is merely to point out a few species, remarkable either for their rarity, the singularity of their conformation, or their efficacy in medicine. The mere systematic classification of herbs and flowers, without a view to their utility, seems to be but a trifling pursuit, an useless waste of time and patience; but when the botanist, by pointing out their various virtues and powers, or their curious and wise construction, can extend the knowledge of simples, or elevate the mind to contemplation, his labors are then dignified by their laudable and eligible ends.

The *ophrys apifera*, or *bee orchis*, is found in the fields about Carisbrooke castle. It flowers in June and July, and then displays a singular and beautiful contrivance of nature for the preservation of the plant. The great importance of the nectary or honey-gland in flowers is manifest; and surprizing care and various devices are found to have been used, in protecting this part from the depredations of those various insects, which are ever on the wing in search of this delicious vegetable liquid. To this end the nectarium of the *bee orchis* is formed with so near a resemblance to the wall bee, as at a small distance to be easily mistaken for that insect; by which appearance, it is probable, a number of depredators, who would otherwise rob the plant of its means of support, are deterred from approaching it.

The *digitalis*, or *fox-glove*, is a most beautiful and shewy wild plant, occurring in almost every hedge-bank hedge-bank in the ifland. It is indeed common to moſt parts of Southern England, and therefore not mentioned here on account of its rarity, but becauſe it teems with efficacious virtues, which are by no means generally underſtood. The misfortune is, that in the vegetable world, as in every thing elſe, we are apt to overlook and deſpiſe thoſe productions which are moſt common, not troubling ourſelves with an inveſtigation of their ſeveral properties; whereas it is not improbable, (reaſoning from the kindneſs of nature in other reſpects) that thoſe which moſt perpetually occur, are moſt replete with medicinal uſes, would we be at the trouble of ſearching them out;

> " But yet the wholeſome herb neglected dies,
> Though with the pure exhilarating foul
> Of nutriment and health, and vital pow'rs,
> Beyond the reach of art 'tis copious bleſs'd."

The ſalutary effects of the digitalis are experienced in one of the ſevereſt maladies that can afflict the human frame; the *anaſarca*, a kind of dropſy, attended with an enlargement of the legs and thighs, and a difficulty of respiration. In this disorder, the following decoction is found to be extremely efficacious, and in a very short time; one large spoonful, or half an ounce, being taken twice during the day.

Boil four ounces of the fresh leaves of purple fox-glove, from two pints of water to twelve ounces; and add to the strained liquor, while yet warm, three ounces of rectified spirit of wine.

The preparation of it is easy, the mode of administering simple, and the good effects nearly certain.* There can be no difficulty in distinguishing this elegant plant from its more homely neighbours; the length of the stem, thickly set with inverted corollas, of a purple hue, and a bell shape, forming a beautiful cone of flowers, sufficiently points it out.†

On

---

* Vide a pamphlet, entitled, "Experiments on Mucilaginous and Purulent Matter," by Dr. Darwin. Cadell, 1780.

† This plant may be further ascertained by the following character. The leaves of the calyx are ovate (egg-shaped) and acute, with the segments of the corolla obtuse

On the Eastern shores of the island is found the *conferva polymorpha*, which receives its name from the singular changes it undergoes in form and appearance. Originally it is of a red hue; this it first discards for brown, and shortly afterwards becomes black; dropping, at the same time, its lower leaves, and lengthening some of its upper ones, to the almost total alteration of its pristine figure.

The *lichen calcareum*, or liver-wort, occurs on all the rocky elevations. This plant seems to be the foundation of all vegetation, drawing its own nourishment probably from air alone, originally. It is the first vegetable that appears on the broad front of the naked rock, which it runs over with a kind of net-work. When it dies away, its recrements afford a bed for other mosses to root themselves in, which in their turn perish, and leave an additional soil for succeeding plants;

---

obtuse, and the upper lip entire: the inside of the corolla is beautifully sprinkled with spots resembling eyes; and the leaves are large and wrinkled. The color of the flower is red. Rousseau's Letters on Botany; Martyn's edit. 1794; p. 316.

thus probably has the globe gradually acquired the means of supporting vegetables, and assumed that soil with which it is covered, from the naked appearance it exhibited after the ravages of an universal deluge.

Among the ledges and precipices of the cliffs is found the *crithmum maritimum*, or rock-samphire; which is gathered for sale by the adventurous hinds of the island. Well might Shakspere pronounce this avocation to be a *dreadful trade;* * for it is a fearful sight even to see the business performed, much more terrible then must the actual execution of it be. The mode is the same with that practised, and before hinted at, in acquiring the puffin eggs; a rope attached to a crow bar firmly fixed on the brow of the cliff, by which the person lowers himself down to the crevices wherein the samphire is found; and by the same means clambers again to the summit, when he has filled the basket girt around him. There is, however, some little fraud practised now and then by these samphire dealers,

* In his King Lear.

dealers, and the purchaser (unless he be a botanist and can discover the deceit) is furnished with a bastard kind of plant, by no means so fit for medicinal or culinary purposes as the genuine samphire. This substituted vegetable is called the *inula crithmoides*, or golden samphire, and gathered, with little trouble and no danger, on all the sea beaches in and near the island. The fallacy may be detected by observing the formation of the plant, and tasting the stalk or leaf. In the genuine samphire, the stalks are succulent, the leaves pinnate (winged, or feathered) formed of three or five divisions, each having as many small, thick, lance-shaped leaves. Both these and the stalk have a pungent taste. In the other species, the stalk, on the contrary, is roundish, jointed, and tasteless; with a tough string running through the middle of it, instead of the flat leaf of the *crithmum maritimum*.*

The submarine rocks and stones which line the coasts of the island, abound with various aquatic plants; such as

---

* Rousseau's Letters on the Elements of Botany; translated by Professor Martyn; edit. 1794; p. 233.

The *fucus fibrosus*, or fennel-leaved wrack or sea-weed;

The *fucus bifidus*, or bifid ditto;

The *fucus caniliculatus*, or furrowed ditto;

The *fucus crispatus*, or branched ditto;

The *fucus albidus*, or white ditto—a very beautiful species;

The *fucus multifidus*, or multifid ditto:

The *ulva purpurescens*, or purple laver;

The *ulva capillaris*, or capillary ditto;

The *ulva filiformis*, or filiform ditto—most of them constructed for riding on the waves, by the assistance of numberless little bladders filled with air, which support them on the surface, and thus enable them to form vast beds of floating vegetation.

The mildness of the climate in this part of England, is manifested by the great numbers of the *myrtus communis*, or common myrtle, to be seen here in all its varieties. It needs no particular culture or attention, but braves the variations of the external air, and all the rigors of the winter; circumstances which would have afforded

forded sufficient hints for ancient mythologists to have ascribed the tutelage of the island to the gentle goddess of love;

"Populus Alcidæ gratissima, vitis Iaccho,
Formosæ *myrtus* Veneri, tua laurea Phœbo."*

* Virg. Eclog. The myrtle flourishes best in a warm marine situation—
"Pallentesque ederas, et amantes littora myrtus.—Virg. Georg. I. verse 28.

CHAP.

CHAP. VI.

OF THE FOSSILOGY OF THE ISLE OF WIGHT.

THE island consists chiefly of an immense mass of calcareous matter, of a chalky nature, running in a direction East and West. Of this all the higher parts are composed; the other flat and less animated spots exhibit a gravelly, sandy, or clayey soil.

This chalk, however, is not of so soft and fine a texture as that found more to the Eastward, by Portsmouth, and along the Sussex downs; approaching nearer to limestone. It is, notwithstanding, dug both for medicinal and agricultural purposes, and used as a manure throughout the whole island.

In

In the pits which have been thus formed, are frequently found chalk-foffils of different forts, fuch as *echini, fharks' teeth,* and *ammoniæ,* that have preferved their form, enveloped in the calcareous matter wherein they were bedded, throughout all the unknown and wonderful mutations it has in the lapfe of ages experienced.*

---

* A modern philofopher thus accounts for the formation of *chalk.* " The limeftone rocks have had their origin from fhells formed beneath the fea, the fofter ftrata gradually diffolving, and filling up the interftices of the harder ones; afterwards, when thefe accumulations of fhells were elevated above the waters, the upper ftrata became diffolved by the action of the air and dews, and filled up the interftices beneath, producing folid rocks, of different kinds, from the coarfe limeftones to the fineft marbles. When thefe limeftones have been in fuch a fituation that they could form perfect cryftals, they are called *fpars,* fome of which poffefs a double refraction, as obferved by Sir Ifaac Newton. When thefe cryftals are jumbled together, or mixed with fome coloring impurities, it is termed *marble,* if its texture be equable and firm; if its texture be coarfe and porous, yet hard, it is called *limeftone;* if its texture be very loofe and porous, it is termed *chalk.*"—Darwin's Bot. Garden, Firft Part, additional notes.

With refpect to *foffil fhells,* it is a very curious circumftance, that many of them are not now known to our naturalifts

The range of cliffs which form the bold Southern shore of the island exhibit also a great variety of beautiful *fossil shells;* amongst which are seen vast and perfect *echini ; cornua ammonis,* of all sizes, from six inches to eighteen in diameter; *cavas ; turbinated* and *bivalved* shells of various species, either now altogether unknown in a living state, or inhabitants only of the tropical climates. They are sometimes found bedded in limestone rock ; and, in other spots, enveloped in a dark-colored, indurated clay, which is soluble by water.

_{naturalists in their recent state ; and that, on the other hand, the shells most numerous in their recent state, are not known in a fossil one. The cornu ammonis, for instance, of which such numbers are every where discovered in the fossil state, has never been discovered in a recent one. " Were all the *ammoniæ* destroyed," says Dr. Darwin, " when the continents were raised? Or do some genera of animals perish, by the increasing power of their enemies? Or do they still reside at inaccessible depths in the sea? Or do some animals change their forms gradually, and become new genera ?" Philosophy may ask these questions, but it is to be feared the narrow bounds of human knowledge will never enable us to give satisfactory answers to them.}

A thick

A thick and extensive stratum of a close, black, earthy stone, or *schistus*, runs under the whole island. It appears at low water mark on the coast near Mottiston. When first taken up it can be penetrated by any sharp or pointed instrument; but after having been sometime exposed to the air, it indurates, and makes very good whetstones. The inhabitants call it *plotmore*.

A stratum of *coal* discovers itself at the foot of Bimbridge cliff, and runs through the Southern part of the island, appearing again at Warden ledge, in Freshwater parish. On the North side of this stratum, lie a vein of white sand and another of fuller's earth; and on the South side is a vein of red ochre. The coal is said to be of a good quality. The late Sir Robert Worsley sunk a shaft at Bimbridge, in order to ascertain the depth of the stratum; but finding it was very thin, he did not conceive the profits of working it would answer the charges of the undertaking, and therefore desisted.*

* Sir Richard Worsley's Hist. p. 7.

Various sorts of *stone* are found in the Isle of Wight, but none of very superior quality. That which was formerly dug near Quarr Abbey, (so named from its neighbourhood to these quarries) appears to have been for several centuries in some estimation; the cathedral at Winchester and other ecclesiastical edifices being built with it. When the Portland freestone, however, once became known, its qualities were found to be so much more valuable than those of the Quarr stone, that the latter sunk into disrepute, soon ceased to be called for, and is now forgotten. There are several varieties of stone also, at the back of the island, but being all of a sandy nature, coarse grain, and dark color, they are not in much request.

The *argilla apyra*, a heavy, ductile, white clay, commonly called *tobacco-pipe clay*, is found in the island; there are several considerable strata of it, which are made to turn to good account.

Amongst the fossil earths of this district, may be reckoned the *argilla fullonica* (fuller's earth);
the

the *argilla marga*, or white marle; the *marga columbina*, or dove marle; the *ochra ferri*, or yellow ochre; and the *ochra Syriaca*, or red ochre: the two laſt are particularly obvious in Alum bay, where their mingled ſtrata form a beautiful and variegated appearance at a ſmall diſtance. At the ſame ſpot is alſo found the *arena micacea argentea*, or white ſilvery ſand, of infinite uſe in the glaſs and porcelain manufactories, for which it is perpetually ſhipping off. The bed of it is, however, ſo immenſe, that ſcarcely any diminution in the quantity can be perceived.

The name of this bay ſufficiently points out the kind of foſſil ſalt produced there. The *alumen commune*, common native alum, is found in conſiderable quantities. As it is a ſalt of great efficacy and uſe both in medicine, dying, &c. the crown uſed formerly to monopolize the whole of it; and proper people were appointed to gather and preſerve it for government. This practice commenced with Queen Elizabeth, who having

learnt

learnt that much of this natural production was to be gotten in the ifland, fent the following mandate to the then governor, Mr. Richard Worfley, in order to afcertain the truth of what fhe had heard, and to avail herfelf of it, if it were fo.

"After my right harty commendacons— Whereas the Quean's Majefty being infermyd that there is w̅t̅ in that Ile certen Oure of Alume. For trial and Profe whereof her Highnefs purtly fendeth thider the Bearer herof one Bendall. Thefe fhall be in her Mat's. Name to require you with your Authorite and fav^r. fo to affift him in that behalf, as he may revyfe fyche partes there as he fhall thynk to be meete for the purpofe and bring w^t. him fume part of the fayde Oure to the End he maye therof make fume profe here w̅t̅ in the Realme. In this part as her Highnefs trufteth, you will give order that no man there fhall impede and refift him; foe he hath charge to ufe himfelf with fyche moderation and refpect of behavior as fhall apperteyne.

And

And thus I bid you hartely well to fare. Fro the Court at Weſtmynſter the 7th. daye of Marche 1561; your aſſured

Frend,
W. Cecil."*

Small maſſes of the *ſulphur vivum opacum*, or *yellow native ſulphur*, are picked up on ſeveral parts of the iſland ſhores; and ſuch quantities of *copperas* about Shanklin, as are ſufficient to freight ſmall trading veſſels, which carry the ſame to the London markets, and there diſpoſe of it to great advantage.

The expectations of the iſlanders were ſome years ſince awakened, on a diſcovery that ſmall particles of *gold* were mingled with the ſand of Chale bay. The circumſtance was ſoon noiſed about, and the whole neighbourhood, filled with the thoughts of ideal fortunes, left their occupations, and bent their attention to the collecting and ſifting of this precious ſand. After a ſhort time, however, the gold duſt ceaſed to appear,

---

* Sir Richard Worſley's Hiſt. Append. No. II.

and

and it was found out, that a Spanish ship having been wrecked on the coast, this rich article, which had been supposed to be the natural production of the place, was part of her cargo, washed ashore by the violence of a ground sea. The islanders therefore returned to their homes and usual avocations, somewhat disappointed, but wisely determining to content themselves for the future with the slow but certain profits of agriculture, and mercantile pursuits.*

* " *Argentum et aurum*," says the incomparable Tacitus, speaking of the natural productions which their country yielded to the Germans, " *propitii an irati dii negaverint, dubito.*" Could our philosopher have beheld the evils which the possession of these fatal metals occasioned to the innocent inhabitants of the *new world ;* or have taken a view of the barbarism, ferocity, and wretchedness which are exhibited on the gold coast, from one extremity to another, he would have entertained no doubt on the subject; but instantly acknowledged the kindness and benevolence of the gods, in denying these " shining mischiefs" to the honest Germans.

A GENERAL VIEW
OF THE
AGRICULTURE
OF THE
ISLE OF WIGHT.

"Χρῃίζων πλετυ, μελιτην εχι πίον☉. αγρυ."*

"Ye gen'rous Britons! venerate the plough,
And o'er your hills, and long withdrawing vales,
Let autumn fpread his treafures to the fun,
Luxuriant and unbounded."

CHAP. I.

A SKETCH OF THE PROGRESS OF AGRICULTURE IN BRITAIN, FROM THE EARLIEST TO THE PRESENT TIMES.

AGRICULTURE is one of the neceffary arts of life; perhaps the moft fo of any other. At leaft it muft be the firft ftep towards comfort and civilization. Whilft men continue to lead

* "If ardent thirft of wealth thy bofom warm,
Leave vain purfuits, *and take a fertile farm.*"—Phocy. Sent.

Mm a wandering

a wandering, unsettled life, without fixed habitations, they will of course remain savage and unenlightened; nor can any scintillation of improvement be expected to appear in their minds and manners, till the knowledge and practice of agriculture have given them ideas of the advantages resulting from the possession of permanent property, and taught them to be stationary, and to settle and associate together.

That the first Celtic inhabitants of this kingdom were not arrived to the knowledge of agriculture, when they wandered hither, has been suggested before; they were in that stage of human manners denominated the *hunter state*, migrating from place to place, without any notions of permanent property or settled abode.

Their Belgic successors, in the South of Britain, had advanced a step beyond these barbarians, and possessed some little theoretic and practical knowledge of husbandry; though so crude and perverse were their ideas on the subject, that they esteemed the pursuit of this useful art ignoble and impolitic; and actually framed institutions to discourage it.

Cæsar

Cæsar tells us, the diet of these people consisted chiefly of milk, flesh and cheese: that none of them possessed any spot of ground which they could call their own: that the chiefs allotted annually a certain proportion of land to each person, which, at the conclusion of the year, was again resumed, and the temporary owner obliged to repair to another spot; a conduct they adopted for the express purpose, as he further informs us, of weaning the people from agricultural pursuits.*

It was under the government of the Romans, that Britain first exhibited a systematic and respectable husbandry; these conquerors shewed a minute and studious attention to every branch of this art. In their hands it became a perfect science; a subject of eulogy to their orators,†

---

* De Bell. Gal. lib. VI. cap. xxii. Tacitus gives an account nearly similar. De Moribus Germ. cap. xxvi.

† "Omnium rerum ex quibus aliquid adquiretur, nihil est *agriculturâ* melius, nihil uberius, nihil dulcius, nihil homine libero dignius."—Cicero de Officiis, I. cap. xlii.—and again; "Ab aratro arcessebantur qui consules fierent

of difcuffion to the literati,* and of defcription to their poets:

"Such things as thefe the rural Maro fung
To wide imperial Rome, in the full height
Of elegance and tafte by Greece refin'd."

Moft of the modes of tillage which are even now in ufe with us, were introduced amongft the natives of Britain by their Roman conquerors; to whom we are indebted alfo for many of the feeds, plants, roots, and flowers, which adminifter to our prefent comfort, luxury, and amufement.†

At

ficrent. Suos enim agros ftudiofè colebant, non alienos cupidè appetebant, quibus rebus et agris, et urbibus, et nationibus rempublicam, atque hoc imperium et populi Romani nomen auxerunt."—Orat. pro Ligaro.

* Varro; Cato; Columella; Pliny.

† We are to thank the Romans for the following feeds, plants, and roots. The radix, or radifh; the afparagus; the cucumber; the lettuce; the melon; the pea; the faba, or bean; the beet root; the fennel; rofemary; and thyme. They alfo added to the parterre the following flowers—the rhos, or rofe; the lilly; the violet: and to the orchard the following fruits—the pear; the damfon; the cherry; the perfica, or peach; the aprica, or apricot;

the

At the time of the Norman conqueft, the agriculture of Britain appears to have been at a very low ebb. But a fmall proportion of land was in tillage; and the chief attention was bent to the grazing of cattle, and the fattening of hogs.* Little encouragement, indeed, could be given to it in the pure feudal ages; the lord of the demefne was too much occupied in conftant warfare, to attend to domeftic concerns; and his miferable vaffal, with every intellectual faculty chilled and depreffed by ignorance, fuperftition, and fervitude, had neither ability, fpirits, nor inclination, to try experiment, or attempt improvement.

A fmall approach to the increafe of tillage was made at the clofe of the twelfth century, when

---

the cidonia, or quince; the morus, or mulberry; the caftanea, or chefnut; the ficus, or fig; the vitis, or vine; the forbus, or fervice; the mefpilus, or medlar. They introduced cider and perry: and laftly, enlarged the *Britifh fauna* by bringing with them, pheafants; pigeons; partridges; pluvialis, or plover; turtur, or turtle dove; pavo, or pea-cock; rabbit; coccyx, or cuckoo. Pliny.

* Vide Domefday Book, paffim.

the

the barons manumitted a number of their vaffals, in order to ftrengthen their caufe againſt the kingly power. Thefe freedmen receiving at the fame time a certain proportion of allodial land, began inclofing their acquifitions; and foon experiencing the fweets of eating the fruits of their own labor, introduced fome fmall tafte for the purfuits of hufbandry.

But the inaufpicious influence of the feudal inftitutions, and the monopolizing fpirit of the church, that fwallowed up nearly a third part of the landed property of the kingdom, ftill operated as conftant checks upon any little fpirit of agricultural improvement, which might otherwife have gotten abroad; and it was not till the reign of Henry VII. (whofe policy dictated a relaxation and diminution of the feudal tenures) when landed property was to be acquired by moſt defcriptions of people, that any general attention was paid to this art. This event, however, being followed, in the fubfequent reign, by a diftribution of the immenfe poffeffions of the ecclefiaftics amongſt the laity, the united circum-

ftances

stances diffused a pretty universal spirit of husbandry, and lucrative improvement; a spirit, indeed, that operated rather too violently. For the new possessors of these lands, wishing to turn their recently-acquired property to the speediest advantage, began, with all expedition, breaking up the numerous commons and waste grounds, which had hitherto afforded subsistence to the *peasantry* of the kingdom. The legislature perceiving that this system was practised universally with increasing ardor, thought proper at length to prohibit it, as it had a manifest tendency to impoverish and destroy that useful description of people.

Since the period of the Reformation, when the vast advantages of agriculture first became generally known and acknowledged, this useful art has been creeping on by a slow, but progressive improvement, till the present time. During this interval of two centuries and an half, several names, high on the roll of literary fame, have, at different times, honored agriculture with their patronage and recommendation;

dation; nor did Bacon, Milton, Evelyn, or Cowley think it unworthy of their occafional lucubrations. But it was left for the prefent age to call in the influence of *government*, to the promotion, encouragement, affiftance, and improvement of the national hufbandry; a great and wife idea, originally fuggefted by a patriot, whofe affiduous labors in the developement of the true fources of national happinefs and wealth, entitle him to the efteem and gratitude of every real lover of his country.*

* Sir John Sinclair, Bart. Prefident of the Board of Agriculture.

CHAP.

CHAP. II.

OF THE DIFFERENT GRAINS SOWN; USUAL COURSE OF CROPS; VARIOUS MANURES, &c.

THE soil of the Isle of Wight being extremely diversified, as we have seen in a former part of this volume, the modes of tillage, kinds of grains, courses of crops, and sorts of manure, will of course be different in its different districts. We will, however, point out, as nearly as possible, the husbandry of each particular part.

The grains chiefly cultivated here are, wheat, barley, oats, pease, and beans.

Of wheat, all the different sorts are occasionally used. In the neighbourhood of the sea, the farmers prefer the *old white-strawed wheat*, for the sensible reason of its being less liable than any other kind to be injured by high winds and tempestuous weather. On the North* part of the island, the red strawed wheat is usually sown; as well as in all the wet, poor lands, because it is supposed to *run more to straw* than any other kind, and of course enables the farmer to provide more fodder for his cattle in the winter.

Of oats, the common sorts are generally sown; though some farmers, particularly in the Eastern parts of the island, are partial to the *Tartarian* kind; but I am informed they seldom answer.

With respect to beans and pease, more or less attention is paid to them, according to the nature and soil of the land.

The following is a statement of the rotation of crops, in various parts of the island.

Towards the Eastern extremity, the common course, on the free, light-working land, is,

---

* By the North of the island is to be understood *all the lands* on the North of the range of hills which intersect the island from East to West; and by the South of the island is to be understood all the lands lying between the said hills and the ocean.

First

First year, - - Wheat;
Second ditto, - - Barley;
Third ditto, - - Clover;
Fourth ditto, - - Wheat.

On the stiff land they have wheat once in *four years* only.

At the Southern part of the island the following course is used:

First year, - - Wheat;
Second ditto, - $\begin{cases} \text{Fallow dunged, and} \\ \text{turnips;} \end{cases}$
Third ditto, - - Barley;
Fourth ditto, - - Clover.

About Steephill we have the following management:

First year, - - Wheat, oats, or pease;
Second ditto, - Barley, with clover; mow it next summer; feed it afterwards; plough it up; and sow it with wheat again.

Near the centre of the island, the rotation is as follows:

First year, - - Wheat;
Second ditto, - - Barley;

Third year, - - Clover;
Fourth ditto, - -- Wheat.

Towards the Weſtern extremity there is this variation in the management of their crops:

Firſt year, - - Turnips;
Second ditto, - Barley;
Third ditto, - - Clover, and ray-grafs;
Fourth ditto, - - Wheat.

The wheat is prepared for ſowing, ſometimes by ſteeping it in ſalt water, and afterwards mixing it with lime; but generally by ſimply mixing with it lime, which has been ſcalded with boiled freſh water.

The medium produce of wheat on the beſt land in the Southern part of the iſland is about twenty-four buſhels per acre; and on the North ſide of the iſland the average may be laid at eighteen buſhels per acre; ſo that the medium produce *throughout the whole diſtrict* appears to be twenty-one buſhels per acre.

The medium produce of oats is twenty-five buſhels per acre in the Eaſtern part of the iſland, and about five and thirty in the Southern and

Weſtern

Western parts. Of barley thirty bushels on the same spots.

The leguminous crops are generally pretty productive; peafe and beans yielding twenty-four bushels per acre in the Eastern parts; and in the Southern and Western parts, the former giving twenty-eight bushels, and the latter thirty-two bushels, per acre.

In preparing their land for wheat, the islanders give three or four ploughings (as the soil requires) to their fallows; and one on breaking up their clover lays. They sow about two bushels and an half per acre. For oats they seldom plough more than once, and sow about four bushels and an half per acre. For barley they give three ploughings, and sow about four bushels per acre.

The grain is in general broad-cast, though some farmers have adopted the drilling system for wheat, barley, and peafe, which is found to succeed very well in the free, light, sandy soils. When this husbandry is practised, they use a small kind of horse-hoes, which are worked by

a man;

a man; thefe, with the affiftance of hand-hoes, and earthing up the ranks, and keeping them clean by women and children weeders, combine to produce profitable crops.

The fyftem of *fallows*, both fummer and winter, is pretty generally followed throughout the ifland; nor will many of the farmers hear of a contrary practice. Much, indeed, has been written and faid on both fides of this agitated queftion; and the favorers of the different modes are equally pertinacious in fupport of their refpective doctrines. It would be difficult therefore to fay which is right *in all points;* but modern philofophy has proved that the fallowift is *wrong in one.* The great argument of the friend to fallows, for leaving his land in a ftate of idlenefs during the winter, has been the fuppofed benefit it received from the

" Etherial *nitre*—
whate'er the wintry froft
Nitrous prepar'd."

It is now, however, well known, that neither ice nor fnow contain any *nitrous* particles, nor in any

any degree *meliorate* the ground; for, according to the obfervation of an excellent natural philofopher, though froft, by enlarging the bulk of moift clay, leaves it fofter for a time after the thaw, yet as foon as the water exhales, the clay becomes as hard as before, being preffed together by the incumbent atmofphere, and by its felf-attraction.* Hence, therefore, one of the ftrongeft reafons for purfuing this fyftem vanifhes into air.

In many of their ftiff clayey lands, the iflanders dibble beans; but fome improvement might be introduced into this branch of huf-bandry. By planting ten pecks upon an acre, (a common practice), a very ufelefs wafte of feed is occafioned; and in not hoeing them when they come up, which in general they omit doing, the plant is lefs healthy and productive than it would be if properly attended to.

Potatoes are not fo much regarded in the Ifle of Wight as their excellence and utility deferve. The little farmers, and laboring poor, are almoft

* Dr. Darwin.

the only people who plant them: the land intended to receive them is fallowed and well dunged, the potatoes (divided according to their eyes) are then planted in rows; the rows being about a foot diſtance from each other; and earthed up when about four or five inches above the ground. In general the crops are very ſatisfactory; from ſixty to eighty ſacks per acre.

I confeſs, I am aſtoniſhed that more attention is not paid to the potatoe, in this part of Hampſhire, where ſo many ſpots are found, peculiarly well calculated for its cultivation. Of all the roots which our climate produces, none perhaps is of greater, or more general uſe than this; whether it be conſidered as a meliorator, cleanſer, and improver of the ſoil, or as a plant which affords a cheap and nutritious food, both to men and to cattle. Viewed in the light of profit alſo, it would aſſuredly anſwer well to the Iſle of Wight farmer to cultivate potatoes, as his vicinity to Portſmouth, whither they might be carried at a trifling expence, would always

inſure

infure him an immediate and profitable market for his crop.

I am confcious, that with many farmers this plant is no great favorite; nor is a crop of potatoes confidered by them as an *improving* one. So far from it, indeed, that in fome counties, about Crewkerne in Somerfetfhire, for inftance, as a very intelligent gentleman has informed me, the landlords reftrict their tenants by fpecial covenants, from planting more than a very fmall quantity of land with potatoes, under the idea of their being very *impoverifhing roots*. However, in this, as well as in moft other matters in agriculture, much muft depend on the nature of the foil, the management and preparation of the land, and the different forts and quantities of manure, &c. made ufe of in different parts.

The times of fowing and harvefting are as follow. Wheat and winter vetches are generally fown in October, and harvefted in Auguft; oats are fown in March; barley, in April; beans, in February; and peafe, in February or March.

March.* Peafe are harvefted in the latter part of July, or beginning of Auguft, and the other grains in September.

Their manures are chiefly chalk and dung arifing from the farm-yard, which, after lying for fome time in a heap, is mixed with earth. From fifteen to twenty pots per acre, of this compoft, are fpread on the lands prepared for wheat. Chalk is alfo much ufed, its durable and improving qualities having been of late years experienced by the Ifle of Wight farmers. They put about one hundred bufhels of it upon an acre, which continue to operate beneficially for fourteen or fifteen years. Some few experimental farmers have of late tried the effects of *fea-weeds* as a manure; and mixing them up with dung, lime, and earth, formed a compoft, and fpread it on the foil: but I am informed their pains have not been, in many inftances, rewarded with fuccefs.

* Some farmers fow their peafe as early as January; and thefe are generally found to produce the beft crops.

In the ifland the farmers have a choice of marles, both ftone and teftaceous: when they find it neceffary to ufe this manure, they ufually put from twenty to twenty-four waggon-loads upon an acre.

The farms are of a moderate fize, fome few under £100 per annum, and fome above £400 per annum; but the general run is between thofe two fums.

Early in Henry the Seventh's reign, a regulation was made for reducing the fize of the farms in the Ifle of Wight, and preventing the landed property getting into the hands of a few individuals, to the decreafe of population, and the deftruction of the peafantry. An act of parliament was paffed, prohibiting any of the inhabitants from holding farms, lands, or tithes, exceeding the annual rent of *ten marks;* an abfurd law, which could not long operate with any efficacy, inafmuch as money was conftantly decreafing in value, and land taking a contrary direction; the confequence of which would be that the fize of the farms muft have been con-

ftantly

ſtantly diminiſhed, to keep them within the letter of the act.

The average *rent* of land on the South ſide of the iſland, including foul ground, does not exceed fifteen ſhillings per acre; and on the North ſide the medium is about eleven ſhillings per acre. Eſtates, when ſold, fetch about twenty-eight years purchaſe.

CHAP.

CHAP. III.

TURNIPS; GRASSES; PASTURE; DRAINING; AND ROADS.

TURNIPS are now highly efteemed in the Southern, Weftern, and central parts of the ifland; and the farmers are correcting an error, which fome few years fince they were guilty of, viz. not hoeing this valuable root. They now plough four times, harrow and hoe once, and feed them off with fheep by hurdling.

The green crops moftly cultivated are, turnips, clover, vetches, ray-grafs, and trefoil. They have alfo fome buck-wheat; but the quantity is fmall, and only raifed in their lighteft and moft fandy foil. It is generally given to the hogs, for the purpofe of fattening them.

Of clover they cut on an average about one ton and an half per acre; and then let it go to feed.

feed. Vetches are now and then fowed after clover, and, according to the pleafure of the farmer, are either fed off, or mowed, and given to the horfes in the ftable.

The pafture and meadow land is extremely rich, and produces from one to two tons of fine hay per acre. The dry meadows are well manured, at the proper feafon, with good rotten dung; and the wet ones kept in excellent order by well-managed drains. The common method of forming thefe drains is by digging a trench, two feet and an half deep, in which fmall picked ftones, or lumps of chalk are thrown to the height of a foot; on thefe is placed a layer of ftraw, heath, or furze; and the whole is then covered with foil. The expence of this operation is about nine-pence per perch.

The *roads* of the ifland (particularly in the Eaftern divifion) are paid great attention to; and, except in the Southern parts, where their natural rocky ruggednefs and inequality cannot be rectified by labor, are as good as thofe of Hampfhire. The Weftern divifion being more thinly
in-

inhabited, the roads here are lefs pleafant to the traveller; though, indeed, of late years, great improvements have been made in thefe means of communication throughout the whole ifland.

They are formed and repaired, as in other places, by the refpective parifhes or tythings through which they pafs.

CHAP.

CHAP. IV.

SHEEP, HORSES, COWS, AND SWINE.

THOSE profitable and useful animals, *sheep*, have been very much attended to of late years by the Isle of Wight farmers, who fully find their account in adopting this excellent system of husbandry.*

---

* It is only since the introduction of the Norfolk husbandry into the Isle of Wight, that the *sheep-farming* has been attended to there; the yeomanry are now fully aware of the many advantages which arise from keeping numerous flocks of these animals, whose uses are thus described by an ancient faunist. " Post majores quadrupedes ovilli pecoris fecunda ratio est; quæ prima sit, si ad utilitatis magnitudinem referas. Nam id præcipuè contra frigoris violentiam protegit, corporibusque nostris liberaliora præbet velamina; et etiam elegantium mensas jucundis et numerosis dapibus exornat."--Columella, de Re Rusticâ, lib. VII. cap. ii. Had the Roman added the *dung* to its other advantages, the catalogue would have been complete.

The

The number of sheep annually shorn is computed to amount to forty thousand. In the year 1793, five thousand lambs were sold to the London butchers alone. And during the summer of that year, when I happened to be at Newport, one of these dealers bought fifteen hundred of them.

The Dorsetshire breed is the one in general use; perhaps however, by occasionally *changing it* (a practice not sufficiently attended to here) that degeneracy might be prevented, which I observed began to appear in two or three flocks. This is a practice common with all the great sheep farmers in the West of England; and, as I have heard some of the most intelligent declare, is the only method of keeping up the original perfection of a flock.

The average weight of wool per fleece, in the Eastern part of the island, is three pounds; and in the Southern and Western parts, about three pounds and an half. Little of this is manufactured in the island, it being chiefly exported in the fleece to different trading towns.

The stock usually kept on the farms consists of sheep, cows, and horses; oxen are rare, what few there are, the farmers generally feed with straw and hay, and work them as horses.

The cows are mostly of the Devon breed, though blended with other sorts. The farmers also make a point of having a few Alderney cows in their dairies, which they think produce a better and sweeter butter than would be made without their milk.

These little animals are extremely profitable, some of them giving to the dairy, during part of the summer, nine and ten pounds of butter per week. It is matter of surprize that this breed is not more generally attended to in other parts of the kingdom, than appears to be the case. The original price of a good Alderney cow, at the place where she is imported, is seldom more than eight guineas; she is equally hardy with our own breeds, nay perhaps has the advantage of them in this respect; consumes less provender, and certainly yields as much milk, the cream of

which

which gives a richness to butter, not observable in what is made from the English cow.

The horses are of different breeds, but in general large, and, I think, black. As there is some emulation among the farmers with regard to the beauty and strength of their teams, the draught-horses are fine animals, and kept in excellent order.

It was the practice formerly among the farmers of the island, not to confine their cattle to the farm-yard in winter. Their own good sense, however, or hints from others, have convinced them of the pernicious consequences of this omission. They now adopt farm-yard foddering in the winter pretty generally, and thereby reap those certain good consequences of the practice, health to their cattle, and a great addition to their farm-yard manure.

The *hogs* are of a breed, I believe, peculiar to the island; at least I do not recollect seeing any of the same in other places. They are large and tall, marked with black spots, and have very deep sides; their bacon is excellent.

The *oxen* and *cows* are fattened with hay and turnips. The *hogs* with peafe and barley-meal. The *sheep* are fed in the winter with hay and turnips.

The dairies produce, in confiderable quantities, a particular kind of fkim-milk cheefe, emphatically called the *Ifle of Wight rock*. It is extremely hard; can fcarcely be cut but by a hatchet or faw; is to be mafticated only by the firmeft teeth; and digefted only by the ftrongeft ftomachs.

CHAP,

CHAP. V.

WASTE-LAND; FORESTS; AND SEA-MUD.

THERE is but little *waste land* in the island, and this chiefly exhibits a sandy soil, which would probably repay the expence of being brought into tillage.

Perhaps, indeed, *Parkhurst* or *Carisbrook* forest, lying in the centre of the island, may at present be properly denominated waste land, as it remains in an inactive, useless state, without affording any advantages to the crown, of whose demesne it makes a part; and very trifling ones to the inhabitants who reside in its neighbourhood. This tract of land, which contains three thousand acres, is situated to the North of Newport and Carisbrook; and though called a *forest*, has long been without a tree of any value. There is, however,

however, a lodge still kept up, and a keeper appointed, whose office it is to preserve the deer and the wood, of which scarce a vestige remains. Notwithstanding the inattention paid hitherto by government to Parkhurst forest, the soil is in many places extremely good, and capable of being applied to the most valuable purposes. Several large spots are to be found on which the oak would thrive surprizingly well, and none are so bad as to preclude the hope of the larch, Scotch fir, and such hardy trees succeeding on them.

The obstacles which present themselves to the plan of inclosing and planting the other royal forests in the kingdom, such as the adjustment of multiplied and complicated claims, &c. would perhaps be gotten over without much difficulty, in the case of Parkhurst forest, should government think proper to appropriate it to the growth of timber; since these claims are but few, and confined to a small number of people, (the *real* ones, I mean, for that of a general right of common for black cattle, exercised by the freeholders

holders of the ifland, appears to be a furreptitious one) and confequently might be fettled with little trouble and expence. Thefe claims confift of a right of common for cattle and fheep; and of turbary, (or turf-cutting) and are attached to the eftates immediately adjoining the foreft.

In the Eaftern parts of this ifland are fome tracts of marfhy ground, covered at high tide by the fea, but left bare on its reflux: the largeft of thefe (the others being inconfiderable) is *Brading haven*, containing about nine hundred acres. Into this the fea flows through a narrow inlet. As early as the reign of Edward I. an idea was entertained that there was a poffibility of recovering this ufurpation of foil, from the fea, and converting it to agricultural purpofes; and accordingly Sir William Ruffel, warden of the ifland at this period, made the attempt, and actually fucceeded in gaining a confiderable number of acres; a circumftance fomewhat remarkable, fo little attention being paid in that comparatively barbarous age, by the feudal chieftains, to any thing connected with agricultural

tural improvement. Further acquisitions were also made in the years 1562 and 1594.

The next and last attempt was of a more extensive nature, the particulars of which, as they are curious in themselves, and may afford useful hints to future adventurers in that line, I shall extract from Sir Richard Worsley's History of the Isle of Wight.

A grant of Brading haven was obtained from King James I. by Gibbs, a groom of the bed-chamber. The owners of the adjoining land contested this grant, which the king was very earnest in supporting. After a verdict obtained in the Exchequer, against the gentlemen of the island, Gibbs sold his share for two thousand pounds, to Sir Bevis Thelwall, a page of the king's bed-chamber, who admitted the famous Sir Hugh Middleton to a share. They employed a number of Dutchmen to inclose and recover the haven from the sea. The first taking of it in cost four thousand pounds, and one thousand pounds more were expended in building a dwelling-house, barn, water-mill; in trenching,

quick-

quick-fetting, and other neceffary works; fo that, including the original purchafe, the total expenditure amounted to feven thoufand pounds. But after all, the nature of the ground did not anfwer the expectation of the undertakers; for though that part of it adjoining Brading proved tolerably good, nearly one half of it was found to be a light running fand; neverthelefs an inconteftible evidence appeared, by the difcovery of a well, cafed with ftone, near the middle of the haven, that it had formerly been good ground. Sir Hugh Middleton tried a variety of experiments on the land which had been taken in, before he fold his fhare, fowing it with wheat, barley, oats, cabbage, and finally with rape-feed, which laft was alone fuccefsful. But the greateft difcouragement was that the fea brought up fo much ooze, weeds, and fand, as choaked up the paffage for the difcharge of the frefh water; and at length, in a wet feafon, when the inner part of the haven was full of frefh water, and a high fpring tide, the waters met under the bank and made a breach. Thus ended

ended this expenfive project; and though Sir John Oglander, who lived in the neighbourhood, confeffes himfelf a friend to the undertaking, which, befide its principal object, tended to render that part of the country more healthy, he declares it as his opinion, that the fcheme can never be refumed to any profitable purpofe.

Sir Bevis Thelwall and his heirs labored to afcribe this accident to other caufes, in order to preferve their claims, and to recover compenfation for their loffes; but the whole affair died away, and the fea ftill continues to overflow Brading haven.

The ill fuccefs of Sir Bevis Thelwall and Sir Hugh Middleton (whofe adventurous exertions deferved a better fate,) feems fufficient to deter any future projector, from rifking fo large a fum as would be neceffary to recover Brading haven from the fea, on a fpeculation that has already terminated fo much to the difadvantage of thofe engaged in it. But fhould any gentleman be bold enough to attempt its embankment a fecond time, he would do well to pay every

attention

attention to the mode adopted by the late Count Bentinck, for fhutting out the fea on his Norfolk eftate; who has fhewn an example almoft unique in this kingdom, of laudable fpirit, unconquerable perfeverance, found judgment, and confummate fkill, in adding to his property upwards of one thoufand acres, formerly overwhelmed by the tides of the ocean.

CHAP. VI.

IMPROVEMENTS AND EXPERIMENTS.

THE improvements introduced of late years in the Isle of Wight husbandry, are chiefly such as have occurred in the preceding pages: the general introduction of large flocks of sheep on the different farms, the adoption of some branches of the Norfolk husbandry, and other smaller matters.

But I cannot help dwelling more particularly upon an experiment, which, as it is connected with agriculture, naturally falls within a view of that agricultural system which is practised in the Isle of Wight.

I allude to Sir Richard Worsley's *vineyard*, at his elegant cottage of St. Lawrence, in the Southern part of the island.

The

The claſſical owner of this charming retreat, having remarked a very ſenſible mildneſs of climate in this part of the iſland, (occaſioned by its lying immediately open to the South, and being ſheltered to the North and Eaſt by a high range of rocky hills, which at the ſame time ſhut out the biting winds, and ſtrongly reflect the rays of the ſun on the ſoil beneath them) determined to attempt the propagation of the vines of Bretagne, the climate of which place correſponded in ſome meaſure with that of Steephill.

For this purpoſe he procured the neceſſary number of plants, of the two grapes called *white muſcadine* and *plant verd*, from which the natives of the North-weſt of France make a light white wine: and at the ſame time hired a Breton to attend to their management and cultivation.

The man began his operations in the early part of the year 1792; having gotten rather more than an acre (in a very ſheltered ſpot) into proper order for the reception of the plants, in the month of March he put them into the ground.

This

This piece of land is divided into several beds, each bed being about twelve feet in breadth; these are separated by foot-paths, for the convenience of a near approach to the vines. The plants themselves are placed in rows, at the distance of a foot and an half from each other.

As this first experiment wore a very encouraging appearance, another piece of ground, rather more to the Eastward, and about an acre and an half in extent, was gotten into order, and a similar plantation made in it, in February 1793. These two plantations comprize together about three acres, and contain seven hundred plants.

The man who has the care of these plantations appears to understand his employment, and keeps the plants in good order: the stem of the vine is about eight inches from the ground, and the earth around it is well hoed and freed from weeds. He does not allow more than two shoots to remain on each stem; these are cut off in the ensuing March, and their place supplied by other young ones. The shoots also are not suffered

to

to run into luxuriance; but kept at the length of two feet, or two and an half. In September 1793, when I had the pleafure of feeing thefe plantations, every vine bore the appearance of health and vigor. There was fome little fruit on two or three of thofe which had been firft planted; but this prematurity was to be attributed to their being fituated near a rock, and receiving the rays of the fun ftrongly reflected from it. The vine-dreffer did not expect any confiderable quantity of grapes till the fourth year after planting. He feemed to entertain no doubt as to the fuccefs of his labors, and affured me he had never before feen fuch ftrong and profperous young plants in any vineyard.

But in order to give any poffible chance to his experiment, Sir Richard has not confined himfelf to one mode of planting only. In a bank within his inclofures (having a flope of about forty-five degrees to the South) he has made a terrace confifting of feven ftages, formed of rough ftones rifing like a flight of fteps, one above another. Againft the perpendicular face of each

ftage

ſtage are placed trellifes, and on them the vines are intended to be trained in the manner of efpaliers. The plants were put in during the month of March, in the year 1793.

With refpect, however, to this mode of propagating vines, it may admit of doubt whether it be likely to fucceed or not, owing to the fmall degree of nourifhment which the plants can poffibly receive as they now ſtand. For although the vine *when mature*, will flourifh where there is little foil, nay where there is apparently no foil at all, among gravel, flints, and rocks, drawing fupport with its minute, but far extending fibres, from fources imperceptible to the human eye; yet, I believe, in its *infant* ſtate, it requires more nutriment, and more room for the extenfion of its tender roots, than it will find where it is at prefent planted.

I cannot clofe this fhort, and, I fear, imperfect account of Sir Richard Worfley's vineyard, without adding every wifh for the fuccefs of an experiment which difplays great public fpirit, and has been attended with confiderable trouble and great expence.

CHAP.

CHAP. VII.

THE POOR; LABORERS; AND RATES OF WAGES.

THE paupers of the island are extremely well regulated and taken care of; a system of management adopted of late years, and well worth being attended to and followed in other districts.

Great abuses having been formerly experienced in the management of the poor, in the different parishes of the island, the gentlemen determined to adopt some mode of remedying the evil; and accordingly, in 1770, a general meeting of the respectable inhabitants was held, in which it was proposed that an act of parliament should be procured to consolidate the poor rates of the several parishes, and to erect a *House of Industry* for the general reception of the paupers.

The propofal being agreed to, a bill was accordingly obtained, and a large building erected on part of the foreft of Parkhurft, eighty acres of which were granted by parliament for this purpofe.

The plan of this extenfive edifice is extremely good, it having every convenience that can tend to render the inhabitants healthy, cleanly, ufeful, and induftrious. It is capable of containing feven hundred people, though there are feldom above five hundred refident paupers; two-thirds of whom are conftantly employed in manufacturing facks for corn, flour, and bifcuit; and kerfeys, ftockings, &c. for the ufe of the inhabitants of the houfe. The profits of thefe operations are applied to the fupport of the eftablifhment, the payment of the intereft due on the money borrowed* for carrying it into execution, and the gradual difcharge of the principal.

The act of parliament indeed provided that for the firft twenty years after the completion of the

* This amounted to £18,000.

plan, half the profits arifing from the labor of the poor fhould be applied to the reduction of the poor rates; and half to the payment of the fum borrowed. It being, however, found, that the reduction thus made in the former was inconfiderable, it was thought prudent to apply the *whole* to the latter purpofe, which has been the cafe for fome years laft paft. This meafure, notwithftanding, though founded in fenfe and reafon, has given difguft to feveral, who are not difpofed to endure a prefent trifling inconvenience, for an eventual permanent good; and they talk loudly of compelling, by a fuit in chancery, an adherence to the letter of the act of parliament.

The *rates* throughout the ifland were not equalized at the time of their confolidation; but, that each parifh might pay its fair proportion to the new eftablifhment, an account was taken of the amount of their poor rates refpectively, for the feven years preceding; and an average being ftruck, this was determined to be the ratio of their future payments, till reductions fhould be made from the profits of the houfe. Hence it is that

Rr 2   -   the

the rates vary confiderably in different parts of the ifland; thus, for inftance, Brading pays two fhillings and three pence in the pound upon two-thirds of the rent; Whitwell two fhillings in the pound, upon the rack-rent; and Frefhwater not more than one fhilling and three pence in the pound.

Every praife is due to the gentlemen of the ifland, for their attention to the regulation of this great eftablifhment; which, at the fame time that it exemplifies the *poffibility*, points out the *mode* of rendering the moft unhappy and ufelefs part of the community, ferviceable to the community and comfortable in themfelves.

I have before remarked the pleafing contraft between the laboring poor of the ifland, and thofe of moft other parts of England.

This their comfortable ftate they chiefly owe to the occafional kindneffes of the farmers, who in general bear a high character for benevolence and generofity to thofe who work under them; and their living in a great meafure upon *potatoes*, a wholefome, nourifhing food, and fufficiently

plentiful

plentiful with them, as every laborer's family has a plantation annexed to his dwelling, ſtocked with this uſeful root. Indeed, without theſe aſſiſtances, they would be ſcarcely able to ſubſiſt, as the rate of wages is but low in the iſland, proviſions dear, and the rents of cottages rather extravagant, being from forty ſhillings to two pounds fifteen ſhillings per annum. They are indeed neat little dwellings, built of ſtone, with a little garden to each, for the accommodation of its tenant.

The rates of wages, as well as hours of work, vary in different parts of the iſland. In Brading pariſh laborers have two guineas for the harveſt month, and their board; eighteen pence per day for graſs-mowing, and their beer; and one ſhilling per day during the reſt of the year, when employed. Their hours of work are, in winter from ſeven to four, and in ſummer from ſix to five.

In the Southern and Weſtern parts they get fourteen pence per day, but give an additional
hour

hour of labor, viz. from five to five in summer, and from seven to five in winter.

The crops, however, of the island are so large, (most of the land being in tillage) that the resident laborers are by no means sufficient for the cutting down and harvesting of them. This dearth of hands is supplied from the Western counties, and between three and four hundred laborers annually pass into the island, a little before harvest, and hire themselves to the different farmers, for the month. The usual wages for this period are two guineas if it be peace, and from forty-five to fifty shillings if it be war time. They have their board also. For the time they are employed before and after the month, they have two shillings per day, food, and liquor.

During the harvest of 1793, there were nearly four hundred Dorsetshire, Devonshire, and Somersetshire men employed in getting in the island harvests; and as a warm press was at that time on foot, a general protection from government was allowed to them, to operate during their

their paffage from their own habitations to the theatre of labor, and back again.*

* Since writing the above, I am informed that an agricultural fociety, on an admirable plan, has been founded in the ifland, having for its objeɛt the improvement of the hufbandry of the diftriɛt. I cannot avoid adding my warm wifhes for its fuccefs and profperity.

Roman Coins.

No. 1.

No. 3.

No. 5.

Roman Coins.

Nº 2.

Nº 4.

Nº 6.

APPENDIX.

A Differtation on Six Roman Coins found in the Ifle of Wight.

"The medal, faithful to its charge of fame,
Through climes and ages bears each form and name;
In one fhort view fubjected to our eye,
Gods, emp'rors, heroes, fages, beauties lie."

THE Roman coins exhibited in the annexed tables were turned up in ploughing a field to the North of Carifbrooke caftle, about fifty years ago; and are now in my poffeffion.

They include a feries of about three centuries; and may be confidered as affording an incontrovertible proof of the prefence of the Romans in the Ifle of Wight.

APPENDIX.

The firſt [No. 1.] is a coin of *M. Vipſanius Agrippa*, the ſon-in-law of the Emperor Auguſtus, by his marriage with Julia, the daughter of Auguſtus and Scribonia. He had early eſpouſed the cauſe of Octavius, and rendered him ſuch ſignal ſervices as ſecured the warm friendſhip and laſting attachment of the young emperor, who, amongſt other inſtances of it, had him thrice appointed to the conſulſhip. It was during the laſt time of his filling this office, that the coin in queſtion appears to have been ſtruck.*

The face of it repreſents the head of Agrippa, encircled with a *roſtral crown*,† a reward he

---

* It may be obſerved that the power of coining money was veſted in the ſenate; hence the initials S. C. or ſenatûs conſulto, by the decree of the ſenate, on the reverſe of moſt of the pieces. It was alſo an uſual compliment, paid by this body to the emperors, or their relations, whenever any thing ſignally glorious or ſerviceable to the ſtate had been performed by them, to ſtamp the circumſtance on coins, and ſend them into circulation, with a few initials expreſſive of it.

† The engraver has made a miſtake, omitting the *roſtrum*, or prow, on the front of the crown, and making it ſimply a laurel chaplet. The roſtral crown was beſtowed on the man who firſt leaped into the enemy's ſhip during the engagement.

received

received from the hand of the emperor in return for his gallantry in feveral fea actions; particularly in one fought with Sextus Pompeius, to which, and its honorable reward, Virgil alludes in the following lines;

"Parte aliâ ventis et diis Agrippa fecundis
Arduus agmen agens; cui belli infigne fuperbum
Tempora navali fulgent roftrata coronâ."*

The neck of Agrippa is reprefented as bare, and the hair fhort and curling. Thefe were fafhions amongft the old Romans, who left both the arms and neck entirely expofed to view; a knowledge of which circumftance throws confiderable light on, and gives additional beauty to that natural picture of jealoufy fo admirably painted by the Roman Poet;

---

* Virgil, Æneid. VIII, et Dio, lib. XLIX, Agrippa was the fecond perfon who received the reward of a roftral crown for his naval prowefs; the learned *Varro* anticipated him in this honor about thirty years before. Pliny, III. ii,.et VII. xxx.

"Cum

"Cum tu Lydia Telephi
  Cervicem roseam, et cerea Telephi
Laudas brachia, væ meum
  Fervens difficili bile tumet jecur."*

"Ah! when on Telephus his charms,
His rosy neck, and waxen arms,
My Lydia's praise unceasing dwells,
What gloomy spleen my bosom swells."†

The reverse of this coin bears the figure of Neptune, holding a trident in his left band, and treading with his contrary foot on a kind of globe.

The coin is of brass, the size of the engraving.‡

* Hor. Carm. lib. I. ode xiii.

† Francis.

‡ The Romans very wisely struck all their devices on the baser metals, for two reasons; that the knowledge of the circumstances they were meant to commemorate might be the more universally imparted; and that covetousness might not annihilate the monument, by defacing the device, and melting the metal. It is to be remembered, that what we call Roman *coins* are nothing more than the common currency of Italy, in the times of the ancients.

No.

No. 2. is a coin of Tiberius Cæsar, who was adopted by, and succeeded Augustus. The unnatural brutality and infamous practices of this disgrace to manhood are too well known, to render any detail of his character necessary. This coin appears to have been struck during his second consulship; in which he obtained, by the permission of Augustus, the title of Imp. or *Imperator*, the *victorious general*, in consequence of his recent successes in Germany; eight years before the birth of our Saviour.

The reverse represents the figure of *Victory*, standing on the *rostrum* of a ship; ornamented, as the ancients represented her, with a pair of wings, and bearing in one hand a chaplet of laurel, and in the other a branch of palm;* the rewards

* *Alatam* quoque fingi pingique solitam ob velocitatem dixeris (quo enim citiùs victoria parta, ac breviori spatio victi fugatique hostes, eo illustrior est ac celebrior;) vel quod mobilis sit, nunc his nunc illis secunda. *Palma* Victoriæ tributa, quod ejus rami, ut auctor est Aristoteles, Plutarchus, Plinius, et A. Gellius, lib. III. Noct. Att. cap. vi. ponderi imposito resistunt, nec premi se patiuntur, imò contra obsistunt. *Corona* datur *laurea*, quia est vinculum, quo et victi hostes alligari solent, aut verius præmium est victori. Ant. August. Dialog. ii. Antiq. Numismat. p. 23.

of thofe who had fignalized themfelves in battle.*

"Adfuit ipfa fuis alis Victoria."†
And winged Victory herfelf was there.

Nor has our own great Poet forgotten thefe appendages of the Goddefs, in his fublime defcription of the Meffiah, when going to the difcomfiture of Satan and his angels:

"He in celeftial panoply all arm'd
Of radiant Urim, work divinely wrought,
Afcended; at his right hand Victory
Sat *eagle-wing'd*; befide him hung his bow
And quiver with three-bolted thunder ftor'd,
And from about him fierce effufion roll'd
Of fmoke, and bickering flame, and fparkles
    dire." ‡

No. 3. is a coin ftruck in honor of *Germanicus*, on a glorious and memorable occafion. The face of it reprefents him in the habit of a Roman foldier, apparently in the act of addreffing a body

* "Lentæ victoris præmia *palmæ*."—Ovid.
† Claud. de Sex. Conf. Honorii.
‡ Paradife Loft, book vi. line 760.

of people: the reverfe exhibits his triumphal chariot, in which he again appears. This laft circumftance marks the time of the medal being coined, which was during the confulfhip of C. Cœlius Rufus, and L. Pomponius Flaccus, in the feventeenth year of the Chriftian æra, when Germanicus received the honors of a triumph, for his victories over the Germans.*

On both the faces of the coin, this hero is terrefented as holding in his left hand a kind of fceptre furmounted with a bird. This is the ftandard or eagle of the nineteenth legion, one of the three that perifhed with the unfortunate Varus, which was recovered during the aufpicious campaigns of Germanicus, againft the barbarians who had deceived and deftroyed that credulous commander.†

Germanicus

* Tacit. Annal. II. cap. xli.

† " Brufteros fua urentes, expeditâ cum manu L. Stertinius, miffu Germanici, fudit; interque cædem et prædam reperit *undevicefimæ legionis aquilam*, cum Varo amiffam."— Tacit. Ann. lib. I. " Ipfe [Germanicus] majoribus copiis
Marfos

Germanicus was the son of Antonia Minor, and Drusus Major, and cut off in the prime of life, by poison, at the secret instigation of the Emperor Tiberius.*

No. 4. exhibits the head of Antonia Minor, daughter of Mark Anthony and Octavia, and mother of Germanicus and the Emperor Claudius. She bore an amiable character, and met with the general fate of superior worth in those days—a violent death; dying by poison during the reign of Tiberius.† The coin was struck when her son Claudius had obtained the sovereignty, in honor of his deceased parent. He is represented, on the reverse, with the close habit

Marsos irrumpit, quorum dux Malovendus, nuper in deditionem acceptus, propinquo loco defossam Varianæ legionis aquilam, modico præsidio servari indicat. Missa extemplo manus, quæ hostem a fronte eliceret, alii, qui terga circumgressi, recluderent humum : utrisque adfuit fortuna."—Tacit. Annal. lib. II.

* Sueton. in Vit. Calig. cap. i. Tacit. Annal. lib. I. et II.

† Tacit. Annal. lib. III.

and

and veiled head of the *pontifex maximus*, or high prieft, (for the emperors were invefted with all the offices of the priefthood) bearing in his right hand a kind of veffel, called a *fimpuvium*, anciently ufed in the facrificial rites.

No. 5. is a coin of the Emperor Vefpafian, ftruck during his feventh confulfhip, in the year of our Lord 76. At this period the empire was bleffed with univerfal peace, the emperor having, in the preceding year, dedicated and furnifhed a temple to that goddefs. Hence the figure of Peace became a very proper fubject for the reverfe of this coinage, and the fenate, (who regulated the mint) by adopting it, paid a noble though tacit compliment to their emperor, through whofe exertions this bleffing had been procured.

The goddefs is reprefented on the reverfe as refting on a pillar, to fhew the duration and fecurity of the empire's quiet. In her right hand
Tt   fhe

she holds an olive branch,* one of her usual emblems:

"Ingreditur, ramumque tenens popularis olivæ."†

In her left a cornucopiæ, expressive of the plenty produced by the arts of peace:

"Interea pax arva colat, pax candida primùm
 Duxit araturos sub juga curva boves;
Pax aluit vites et succos condidit uvæ,
 Funderet ut nato testa paterna metum;
Pace bidens vomerque vigent—"‡

"Quæ cornu retinet divite copiam."§

* "In aliis plurimis virgo est, [pax] altera oleæ ramum, altera gestans cornu copiæ. Virgo est, ut simplex et integra; clara pacis argumenta. Bello namque virgines contra jus stuprantur ac rapiuntur. Olea signum est pacificatoris, ut legati teste Virgilio. In cornu copiæ obserues spicas, uvas, aliosque fructus, cum vomere, omniaque in hoc cornu, quod Acheloi fuit, cùm in taurum mutatus Herculem superare conabatur; qui alterum fregit cornu, quod Nymphæ acceptum floribus et pancarpio, ut Naso fabulatur, implêrunt."—Ant. Augustini Dialog. ii. Antiq.

† Ovid, Metam. line 7.

‡ Tibullus, El. X. line 1.

§ Seneca, Trag. in Medeâ, de pace.

It

It may be obferved alfo that the flowing veft of the figure appears to be gathered or tucked up before. This feems to be intended, by the Roman mint-mafters, who had a meaning in every thing, to convey a ftronger idea of the abundance produced by a ceffation from war; for we are to imagine this fold of the garment filled likewife with the gifts of Ceres and Pomona, according to the defcription of Tibullus:

" At nobis, pax alma, veni, fpicamque teneto,
Perfluat et pomis candidus *ante finus*."

The fixth and laft coin is one of Galerius Valerius Maximianus, who, from a very bafe origin, was raifed to the purple, jointly with Conftantius, in the year of our Lord 304. He was remarkable for his propenfity to every vice which could difhonor our nature; and an inflexible diflike to the Chriftian religion, which he perfecuted with the utmoft rigor. The ancient fathers of the church affure us his punifhments for his iniquities commenced even in this life, by the vifitation of a tedious, horrible, and loathsome disease, of which he at length expired, hateful to himself and detested by all around him.*

The reverse bears the figure of the *genius* of the empire, holding a *patera*, or sacrificial plate, in his right hand, and a cornucopiæ in his left; for such was the fanciful superstition of the Romans, that they not only believed each individual had his own particular genius or dæmon; but that kingdoms, states, and cities possessed a similar advantage, every one having a presiding intelligence, perpetually employed in averting evil and inducing good.†

* Eusebius, lib. VII. cap. xv.

† "Varios custodes urbibus mens divina distribuit. Ut animæ nascentibus, ita populis fatales genii dividuntur."— Symmachus.

A Copy of the Rate made March 17th, 1653, for the Maintenance of the Minister of Newport. Vide page 119.

WHEREAS this towne and Borough is become very populous, consisting of two thousand five Hundred Souls and upwards, and the Church or Chappell thereof is not endowed wth. any means or Maintenance for the subsistence or livelyhood of any Minister, or Ministers, to preach the word of God, or officiate therein as a minister, or ministers; By means whereof all Godly ministers are utterly discouraged to take the Care and Burthen of the said place and people upon themselves, to the great damage and eternall hazard of the Soules of the poore inhabitants of this same towne. The wch. the Mayor and chief Burgesses of this Burrough are willing, as much as in them lyeth, to remove, redresse, and for the future p'sent, it being a duty incumbent on all magistrates, and therefore have

thought

thought fitt, to conſtitute, ordeyne, and appoint, and do hereby at this pſent aſſembly, conſtitute, ordeyne, and appoint, That for and towards the maintenance of ſuch miniſter, or miniſters, as are, or ſhall be thought fit, and appointed to officiate in the aforeſaid church or chappell, a rate, Tax, or Aſſeſſment, not exceeding the ſome of one ſhilling and ſixpence upon every pound, for one whole yeare, be made on all the Lands and Ten^{ts}. lying wthin the ſame Borough, and alſo on all the Rents and perſonall Eſtate, and Eſtates, of all the Inhabitants, reſiding wthin the aforeſaid Burrough, with reſpect to their beſt abilities in that behalfe, by the Mayor, and the chiefe Burgeſſes of the ſame Burrough, or the Major Part of them, together wth. Eight, ſix, or four of the able Inhabitants reſideing withing y^e ſame Burrough. And that thoſe for the ſame purpoſe ſhall be from time to time elected, named, and choſen by the ſaid Mayor, and chief Burgeſſes for the time being, for that purpoſe.*

* Sir R. Worſley's Hiſtory, Append. No. XLIV.

ERRATA.

PAGE	LINE	FOR	READ
99,	5,	riselefs,	uselefs.
101,	5,	natural,	nature.
171,	2,	twelve,	ten.
192,	8,	crush,	crash.
216,	18,	difes,	difcs.
228,	21,	στοργη,	στοργη.
232,	16,	ditto,	ditto.
265,	7,	μελιτην,	μελιτην.
268,	3,	things,	themes.

INDEX.

A

	PAGE.
ABORIGINAL Inhabitants of Britain	1
their favage ftate	3
Anecdote from Strabo *(note)*	5
Arthur, prince of the Silures, oppofes the Saxons	19
Adelwalch, king of the South Saxons, receives the ifland	22
Alfred defeats the Danes	25
Adam de Gordon, warden of the ifland	38
Affeton, Sir Richard de, warden of ditto	38
Annebout, the French admiral, invades the ifland	44
Alfred, his political regulations	55
Artillery provided by the inhabitants of the ifland	75
Arreton church, an account of	116
Ancient connection between the ifland and the continent	186
Aquatic fowl	199
Ammodytes, or fand-eels	218
Animal στοργη, inftances of	228

U u

INDEX.

Anasarca, recipe for	250
Ammoniæ	257
Argilla apyra	260
fullonica	260
marga	261
Arena micacea argentea	261
Alumen commune	261
Alderney cows	290

B

Belgæ, who they were	3
when they arrived in England	3
Britons of Belerium (or Cornwall) trade with the Phœnicians	5
Britons send ambassadors to Rome for assistance	17
Bede's account of Saxon devastations *(note)*	18
Bernwinus receives charge of fourth part of the island	22
Baldwin de Redvers, lord of the island	30
Barons, their ancient state	34
Beacons in the island, their number and situation	59
Bishop Wilfred receives a fourth part of the island	95
Brading church, an account of	112
Binstead church, ditto	117
Brixton parish, ditto	124
Brooke church, ditto	126
Borough of Newport	129, 130
of Yarmouth	129
Boroughs, their nature in early times *(note)*	133
Baldwin de Redvers grants a charter to Yarmouth	140
Bray, Sir Reginald, lessee of the island	159

Bolton, Duke of, governor of the ifland	164
Charles, Duke of, ditto	165
Harry, Duke of, ditto	166
Bonchurch, or St. Boniface, fcenery about it	191
Black-gang chine	196
Badgers not found in the ifland	204
Bernard, or hermit-crab	223
Bee orchis	248
Brading haven	295

C

Celtæ, the original inhabitants of Britain	1
migrated hither from Gaul	2
Carifbrook, its probable derivation *(note)*	4
Cornwall, Phœnicians trade thither	5
produces tin	5
Caffiterides iflands, why fo called *(note)*	5
Cæfar, his expeditions into Britain	8
Claudius in Britain	8
Commercial occupations, their effect on the mind	9
Carifbrook, the fite of a Roman ftation	11
Cerdic and Cinric conquer Ifle of Wight	19
Cerdic dies	20
Ceadwalla, king of Weffex, conquers the ifland	22
his cruelty and vow	22
Carifbrook caftle attacked by the French	42
Charles I. his caufe befriended by the Ifle of Wight gentlemen	49
Countefs of Portland, her gallantry	50, 51
Culpeper, Lord, governor of the ifland	52

INDEX.

Carifbrook caftle, ftores of, in Henry the Eighth's reign	70
Caftle of Sandham bay, ditto	71
Caftle at Weft Cowes, ditto	72
Camden's character of the inhabitants of the ifland	76
Culpeper, Lord, governor of the ifland	84
Chriftianity introduced into the ifland	91
Converfion of the Saxon inhabitants of the ifland to Chriftianity	95
Cynbreth, Abbot of Reodford or Redbridge, anecdote of	96
Chriftianity, its depraved ftate in the middle ages	99, 100
Carifbrook priory founded	101
granted to the abbey of Lyra	102
Chapels, feveral in the ifland	110, 111
Carifbrook church, an account of	120
Canteria Manerii de Gatcombe	121
Chale church, an account of	122
Calbourn church, ditto	125
Charles II. grants a charter to Newport	130
vifits Yarmouth	145
Carey, Sir George, governor of the ifland	161
Culpeper, Lord, ditto	163
Cutts, Lord, ditto	164
Cadogan, Lord, ditto	165
Climate of the Ifle of Wight	168
Culver cliff	189
Columba faxatilis, or rock-pigeon	189
Cuttle-fifh	216, 217
Crabs, large	224
Cormorant, hiftory of that bird	239

Conferva polymorpha - - - - 251
Crithmum maritimum - - - - 252
Chalk - - - - - - 256
Coal - - - - - - 259
Clover - - - - - - 286
Cows - - - - - - 290
Cheefe - - - - - - 292

D

Danish tumuli in the Isle of Wight *(note)* 9
Degeneracy of the Britons when deserted by
    the Romans - - - - - 16
Danes, particulars respecting them - - 24
    make a descent on the island - - 25
De Redvers, family of, lords of the island 29, 30
Defence of the island under its lords - 55, 56
    in the reign of Edward I. 57, 58
    in the reign of Edward III. 60-64
    in the seventeenth century 81-83
Druidism the ancient religion of the island - 87
Dimensions of the Isle of Wight - - 168
Downs of ditto - - - - - 180
Dunnofe promontory - - - - 191
Digitalis - - - - - - 248

E

Eastern coast, when first peopled - - 2
Expeditions of Cæsar into Britain did not amount
    to a conquest of the country - - 8
Edward I. purchases the lordship of Isle of Wight 34

Emgiration from the ifland in fourteenth century 41
Eaft-Meden, watches in it in 1638 - - 81
Echo, a remarkable one - - - 194
Eagle, Job's fublime defcription of it - 226
    builds occafionally in Culver cliff - 227
    anecdote of one - - - - 229
Echini - - - - - - 257

F

Fortibus, William de, Earl of Albemarle - 34
French invade the Ifle of Wight - - 40
    attack Carifbrook caftle - - 42
Forts built in the ifland by Henry VIII. - 44
Feudal fyftem, its principles - - 55
Fire-arms introduced into the ifland - 74
Fitz-Ofborne, William, founds Carifbrook priory 101
Frefhwater church, an account of - - 128
Fortibus, Ifabella de, grants charter to Newport 133
Francheville, ancient name of Newtown - 135
Female inhabitants of the ifland - - 179
Fairy rings, their caufe - - - 182
Frefhwater bay - - - - 196
    cavern - - - - 198
    cliffs - - - - 199
Foxes not found in the ifland - - 204
Falco nifus - - - - - 231
Fox-glove - - - - - 248
Foffil fhells - - - - - 258
Fallowing fyftem - - - - 278
Farms, their fize - - - - 283

G

Galatæ or Gauls, the original inhabitants of Britain   1
Gomerians, or Phrygians, Celtæ defcended from them   2
Gallia Belgica, the country of the Belgæ -   3
Godwin, Earl, makes a defcent on the ifland   26
Gallantry, inftance of, in the iflanders -   44
Godfhill church, an account of - - 115
Gatcombe church, ditto - - - 121
Gate, Sir Jeffery, captain of the ifland - 158
Game of the ifland preferved by E. Horfey, Efq. 160
Growth of downs - - - - 181
Gryllus talpa, or mole-cricket, its hiftory   210, 211
Guillemot, hiftory of that bird - - 238
Game, regulations refpecting it by Henry VIII. 242
Gold - - - - - 263

H

Hengift and Horfa, Saxon chiefs, land in England   17
Haftings, battle of, when fought - - 27
Hereford, Earl of, lord of the Ifle of Wight   28
Henry VIII. builds forts in the Ifle of Wight   44
Harby, the feditious curate of Newport - 50
Henry VIII. builds forts on the coaft of the ifland   66
Holmes, Sir Robert, governor of the ifland - 85
   builds a houfe at Yarmouth
to accomodate Charles II. - - 145
Humphrey, Duke of Gloucefter, warden of the
   ifland - - - - - 157
Horfey, Edward, captain of the ifland - 160

INDEX.

Henry, Earl of Southampton, captain of the Isle
  of Wight - - - - 161
Hammond, Colonel, governor of the island - 162
Holmes, Lord, ditto - 166
Hares, plenty of them in the island - - 205
Hermit-crab - - - - 223
Hawks in Culver cliff - - - 230
Horses - - - - - 291
Hogs - - - - - 291
House of Industry - - - - 305

I

Isle of Wight, when first peopled - - 2
  when peopled by the Belgæ - 4
  tin staple removed thither - 6
Ictis, ancient name of Isle of Wight - - 6
Isle of Wight subdued by Vespasian - 9
  conquered by the Saxons - 19
  its inhabitants murdered - 20
  laid waste by Wulpher - 22
  given to Edelwalch - - 22
  annexed to the kingdom of Wessex 22
  its population in the seventh century 23
  its state and appearance under the
   Saxons - - - 24
  attacked by the Danes - - 25
  attacked by Earl Godwin and his son
   Tosti - - - 26
  conquered by the Normans - 27
  given to William Fitz-Osborne 28
  granted to Richard de Redvers 29

Isle of Wight descends to Isabella de Fortibus 33
           purchased by Edward I. - 34
           invaded by the French - 40
           ditto - - - - 42
           ditto - - - - 43
           ditto - - - - 45
           its defence under its lords - 55, 56
           ditto in the reign of Edward I. 57, 58
           its ancient religion - 87—92
Inhabitants of the island - - - 175

J

Jutes, a German tribe - - - 19
Jerom, Earl of Portsmouth, removed from the government of the Isle of Wight - - 46
James I. incorporates Newport. - - 130
          Yarmouth - - 140
John Fitz-Thomas, warden of the island - 155
John de Langford, ditto - - - 156
Job's description of the eagle - - 226

K

Kentish shore first peopled - - - 2
Κασσιτιρος, the Greek name for tin (note) - 5
Kent, kingdom of, established - - 18
King John signs Magna Charta - - 31
     retires to the Isle of Wight - 32
Kingston church, an account of - - 121
Knighton court, ditto - - - 149
Knowles, grand scenery there - - 195

L

Lenity of the Romans to conquered nations	10
Londinium, or London, tin staple removed thither	11
Lords warden of the island, their rights	147
Lymington, Viscount, governor of the island	165
Laboring poor of the island	176
Luccomb, scenery about it	191
Loligo, or cuttle-fish	216
Launce, or sand-eel	218
Limpets	222
Lobsters, of large size	224
Lichen calcareum	251

M

Marseillese Greeks discover Phœnician trade here	6
Marseillese Greeks, when they began to traffic in Cornwall	6
Marseilles, tin sent thither	6
Magna Charta signed by King John	31
Moses Read, the seditious mayor of Newport	49
Military character of the islanders in sixteenth century	76
Militia of the island, the present, when established	85
Monasteries, the original principle of their foundation	100
Motteston church, an account of	124
Montagu, Duke of, governor of the island	165
Medina river	174

Mole-cricket, its hiftory - - 210, 211
Mytilus edulis, or eatable mufcle - - 220
Myrtles - - - - - 254
Marga columbina - - - - 261
Manures - - - - - 282

N

Narbonne, tin tranfported thither - - 6
Normans conquer England - - - 27
Newtown, village of, burnt - - - 43
Northwood, a religious houfe there - - 110
Newchurch church and parifh, an account of 114
Niton church, ditto - - - 115
Northwood church, ditto - - - 117
Newport church, ditto - - - 118
Newtown chapel, ditto - - - 125
Newport borough - - - 129, 130
— when firft regularly fends members
to parliament - - - - 131
Newtown borough - - - - 135
contefts about the elective
franchife there - - - 137–139
Northern coaft of the ifland, its defcription - 188
Needle rocks - - - - - 201

O

Oratory of Burton founded - - - 105
its ftatutes - - 106
granted to Winchefter college - - - 108

INDEX.

Orde, Right Honorable Thomas, governor of
the ifland - - - - - 166
Ophrys apifera - - - - 248
Ochra ferri - - - - - 261
 Syriaca - - - - 261

P

Phrygians, or Gomerians, Celtæ defcended
 from them - - - - 2
Phœnician navigators trade to Britain - 5
 commerce declines here - - 6
Policy of the Romans with refpect to conquered
 nations - - - - - 13
Picts and Scots, their depredations - - 17
Population of the ifland in the feventh century 23
Petition of the inhabitants of the ifland in favor
 of Jerom, Earl of Portland - - - 46
Perfecution of Druidifm by the Romans - 90
Priory of Appuldurcombe founded - - 108
Priory of St. Crofs given to Winchefter college 109
Portland, Earl of, captain of the Ifle of Wight 162
 Jerom, Earl of, ditto - - 162
Portfmouth, Earl of, ditto - - - 166
Polecats not found in the ifland - - 204
Porpeffes - - - - - 214
Pifum, or pea-crab - - - - 221
Patella vulgata, or common limpet - - 222
Puffin, hiftory of - - - 231-233
Plotmore - - - - - 259
Potatoes - - - - - 280
Parkhurft foreft - - - - 293
Poor rates - - - - - 307

Q

Queen Elizabeth increases the British marine	45
Quarr, abbey of, founded by Baldwin, Earl of Devon	103
taxation of its lands in the fifteenth century	104
dilapidated	105
the abbot of, warden of the island	156

R

Romans in Britain	8
lenient to conquered nations	10
acquire the Isle of Wight	11
Roman coins found in the island	12
Romans entirely forsake Britain	17
Roger de Breteville, lord of the Isle of Wight	28
rebels, is imprisoned, and loses his property	29
Richard de Redvers receives a grant of the island	29
Regulations for internal defence of the island	39
Russel, Sir Theobald, slain by the French	40
Religious tenets of the Saxons	92, 93
Richard de Redvers, founder of Appuldurcombe priory	108
grants charter to Newport	131
Richard de Affeton, warden of the island	155
Rivers of the island	174

Razor-fish - - - - - 219
Razor-bill, hiftory of that bird - - 235
Rock-famphire - - - - 252
Roads - - - - - 286

S

Southern coaft of England, when firft peopled 2
Strabo, an anecdote from - - - 5
Scilly iflands, why called Caffiterides *(note)* - 5
Spirit of freedom extinguifhed by luxury - 14
Saxons land in England - - - 17
    conquer Britain - - - 18
Shower of blood falls in the Ifle of Wight *(note)* 30
Sandown fort - - - - 66
    eftablifhment of, in fixteenth century 67
Sharpnode block-houfe - - - 69
Strength of the ifland in 1625 - 77—80
Saxons, their fyftem of religion - 92, 93
St. Helen's priory, when founded and by whom 108
Shanklin chapel, an account of - - 113
St. Boniface church, ditto - - - 113
St. Nicholas chapel, ditto - - - 120
Shorwell church, ditto - - - 123
Shalfleet church, ditto - - - 126
Sir John Lifle, warden of the ifland - - 155
Sir Henry Ties, ditto - - - 156
Sydenham, Colonel, governor of the ifland - 163
Stanley, Hon. Hans, ditto - - - 166
Soil of the ifland - - - - 170
Springs of the ifland - - - - 174
Sandown bay - - - - - 190

INDEX.

Shanklin chine	191
Steephill, rude scenery of	192
St. Catherine's, ditto	195
St. Christopher's cliff	200
Sharks, occasionally on the shores of the island	213
Sand-eel	218
Siliqua, or razor-fish	219
Shells	223
Swallows	245
Submarine plants	254
Stone	260
Sulphur	263
Sheep	289

T

Tin produced in Cornwall	5
purchased by the Phœnicians	5
the derivation of its name *(note)*	5
staple removed to the Isle of Wight	6
Tacitus quoted *(note)*	8
Tumuli in the island	9
Tacitus quoted *(note)*	9
Tin-staple removed from the island to London	11
Tacitus quoted *(note)*	12
Tiberius, coins of that emperor in the island	12
Thanet, isle of, Saxons first land there	17
Tosti, Earl, makes a descent on the island	26
Tyrrel, Sir Hugh, slain by the French	42
Tenure of land, terms of it in the thirteenth century	59
Tenets of the Druids	88
Thorley church, an account of	127

Theobald Ruffel, warden of the ifland - 156
Timber of the ifland - - - 171
Tobacco-pipe clay - - - - 260
Turnips - - - - - 285

U and V

Veneti of Gaul employed in tranfporting tin - 6
Vefpafian's fucceffes in Britain - - 9
   conqueft of the Ifle of Wight - 9
Vectis, or Vecta, Roman name for Ifle of Wight 11
   view of it under Roman government 13
Vernun, William de, lord of the Ifle of Wight 31
Undercliff, a land-flip - - - 193
Vipers in the ifland - - - 206
   their hiftory - - 207, 208
Vineyard, Sir R. Worfley's - - - 300

W

Withgar receives the Ifle of Wight from Cerdic 20
   murders all the remaining Britons in it 21
   calls Carifbrook, Withgarifburg - 21
Wulpher lays wafte the ifland - - 22
Wilfred, Bifhop, receives a fourth part of the
 ifland - - - - - 22
William the Conqueror acquires England - 27
William Fitz-Ofborne receives the Ifle of Wight 27
Worfley's tower built - - - 66
Weft-Cowes caftle built - - - 67
   its eftablifhment in fixteenth
 century - - - - - 67
Watches and wards kept in the ifland in 1638 81

INDEX.

Weſt Meden, watches kept there in 1638	82
Whitwell church, an account of	114
Weſt Cowes chapel, ditto	118
Walleran de Ties, conſtable of the Iſle of Wight	155
William Ruſſel, warden of ditto	155
Worſley, Sir James, captain of the iſland	159
Richard, ditto	160
Webb, General, governor of the iſland	164
Worſley, Rt. Hon. Sir Richard, ditto	166
Woods, the largeſt in the iſland, where	174
Wootton river	174
Woodcocks	244
Wheat	273
Wages	309

Y

Yarmouth, town of, burnt by the French	43
caſtle built	66
caſtle, ſtores belonging to it in Henry the Eighth's reign	68
Yeomanry cavalry of the iſland, when eſtabliſhed	85
Yaverland church, an account of	113
Yarmouth church, ditto	127
borough	129, 140—144
Yar river	174
Yeomanry of the iſland	176

FINIS.

www.ingramcontent.com/pod-product-compliance
Lightning Source LLC
Chambersburg PA
CBHW020225240426
43672CB00006B/417